365

Things to Make and DO

365
Things to Make and DO

Vivienne Bolton

p

This is a Parragon Publishing Book

This edition published in 2004

Parragon Publishing, Queen Street House, 4 Queen Street, Bath BA1 1HE, UK

Copyright © Parragon 1998

Produced by Miles Kelly Publishing Ltd

British Library Cataloguing-in-Publication Data
A catalogue record for this book is available from the British Library

ISBN 1-40543-690-5

Printed in China

The publishers would like to thank Inscribe Ltd., Bordon, Hants. for providing
the art materials used in these projects and
Sophie Boulton for her assistance.

365
Things to Make and DO

Contents

How to Use this Book

This book is filled with ideas for hand-crafted models, toys, useful gifts, and games. You will need a sturdy pair of scissors and good PVA glue, tape, and a set of paints. Most of the crafts can be made from recycled materials from around the house. Some projects are made using natural materials such as twigs, leaves, and pebbles. It is a good idea to save empty boxes, attractive pieces of colored paper, and other useful items for future use.

The introduction will be full of interesting information and inspirational ideas for further projects.

Each project has a list of things that you will need. Check through the list before you begin to make sure you have all the materials and equipment ready.

All the photographs in this book have been carefully taken to illustrate as many ideas as possible.

CANDY JAR AND PLA

Bottle Gar

Create a miniature oasis in a bottle. All you need to start a bottle garden is a large, empty sweet jar and some potting compost. Choose plants which will stay quite small; ask for assistance at your local garden center or florist. Some garden centres have bottle garden departments where they sell small plants suitable for this enclosed, small environment. Bottle gardens should never have the sun shining directly

onto them (the
they do need to
the soil moist. Y
often if the lid is
bottle garden eve
summer. Decora
outliners. Choose
pattern or use bla
paint to create a s
exterior of the bo

You will need:
Sticks
Old spoon
Wire
Kitchen sponge
Cotton wool
A large empty sweet jar
Pebbles or gravel
Suitable potting compost
Suitable plants
Glass paints outliner
Glass paint

The icon at the top of each page tells you what topic is being covered. Here the acorn tells you this is a nature project.

Step-by-step instructions will guide you through each project.

Some of the projects have a Tips and Warnings box. Read these at the start of the project.

ens

...et too hot), but
...ght situation. Keep
...t need to water
...ly on. Feed your
...eeks during the
...glass paints and
...tliner for a stylish
...r and coloured
...s effect on the

1 Begin by making some suitable bottle garden tools. For a digging tool, use an old spoon attached with wire to a long stick. Use a piece of kitchen sponge wired onto a stick to press the earth down when you are planting. Lastly, you will need a cleaning tool. For this use a piece of cotton wool wired onto a stick (you may need a few of these to tidy up the bottle garden once it is planted).

2 Place a thin layer of pebbles or gravel in the base of the bottle. This will provide drainage for the bottle garden plants.

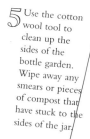

3 Cover the pebbles with a thick layer of potting compost. Press the compost down gently using your sponge tool.

4 Use the digging tool to place individual plants in position. Press the compost down firmly around the plants, taking care not to damage their roots.

5 Use the cotton wool tool to clean up the sides of the bottle garden. Wipe away any smears or pieces of compost that have stuck to the sides of the jar.

6 Your bottle garden is now ready to decorate. Choose a simple pattern and mark it out with the outliner. The stained glass effect will resemble a mini-conservatory.

When choosing plants for your bottle garden choose low growing varieties. Keep the compost moist but do not overwater. Feed your bottle garden every two weeks in the growing season.

Nature

Seedpod Jewelry

C ollect seedpods and hollow stalks from the garden in the summer, and stand them up in a jar to dry in a warm airy spot. You will need a large darning needle to make a hole through the seedpods once they have dried. The beads in the necklaces are made from cut lengths of dried stalks. Thread them using the darning needle and decorate them with paint. Gold and brown paint have been used on these beads to accentuate the natural look. Beads painted in bright colours and decorated with glitter would make an attractive necklace.

You will need:

Selection of seedpods and stalks

Scissors

Paint

Paintbrush

Darning needle

Thread

Felt-tip pens

Rubber band

Check with an adult before you pick plants and stems to dry.

1 To make this necklace you will need a few dried hollow plant stems, some small fir-cones and seedpods. Begin by cutting the plant stems into bead-size lengths. Paint the bead lengths, fir cones, and seedpods gold. When your beads are dry, use the darning needle to make suitable holes through them and thread together using one seedpod to every three plant stems to make a necklace or bracelet.

2 This delicate looking necklace is made simply from some dried hollow plant stems. Once you have cut the stems into bead-sized lengths, decorate the beads using brown felt tip pens or brown paint. Thread them together using the darning needle.

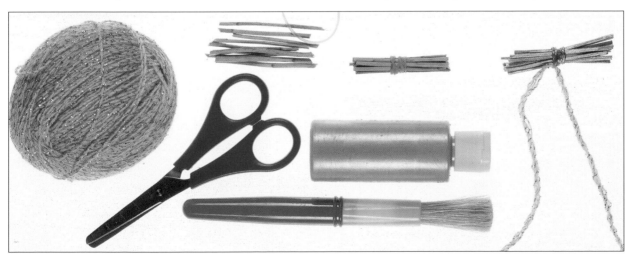

3 A small bunch of twigs is used to make this pendant. Choose straight twigs that don't have any thorns or snags. Use a rubber band to hold them together in a neat bunch to form a pendant. Paint the pendant gold; it may be necessary to give it two coats. Once the paint had dried attach a length of thread to the pendant and it is ready to wear.

OVEN-BAKE CLAY
Birdbath

This mosaic bird-bath would make a good rainy day project. You could use bought miniature tiles or make your own from oven-bake clay like we have. If you make your own tiles you will need to work out the number needed plus a design and color scheme. You could take some inspiration from the color scheme in your garden. Use a tin bowl with a wide lip or ledge for the mosaic pattern. Broken china plates can be recycled to use as mosaic decoration, but ask an adult to assist as the edges can be quite sharp. A mosaic decorated plate would also look good as a houseplant saucer.

You will need:
Oven-bake clay

Rolling pin and knife

Metal plate

Plastic gloves

Spatula

Grout

Cloth

Varnish

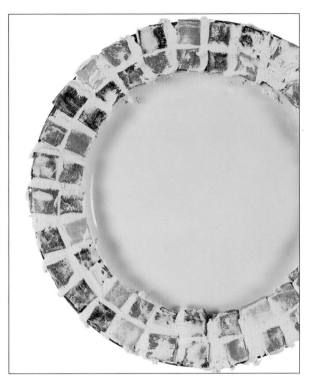

1 Begin by making the tiles using oven-bake clay. Roll out the clay on a clean work surface with the small rolling pin. Cut square tile shapes in your chosen colours to fill the rim of the plate. Harden the tiles in the oven according to the manufacturer's instructions.

4 When the grout has set use the spatula to fill in with more grout between the tiles. Check that it finishes neatly at the edges and allow it 24 hours to dry.

2 When the tiles are ready, make a rough plan of how you will lay them on the plate edge. You will need a metal or china soup plate with a wide raised edge. Put on the plastic gloves and use the spatula to spread a layer of tile grout across the edge of the plate.

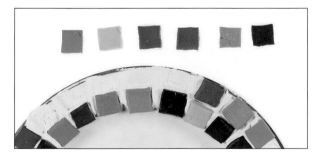

3 Press each tile gently into the grout. Leave a narrow space between each tile. You will fill this later. Make sure the tiles all lie neatly along the edge of the plate. Leave to set for 24 hours.

5 You will now need a cloth to wipe off any excess grout and polish up the tiles. When the tiles look clean, apply a layer of varnish to give them a shine. Let's hope the birds enjoy their new birdbath!

Plate Gardens

While away a rainy afternoon making a miniature garden. These realistic-looking gardens are laid out on dinner plates. You could create an imaginary garden or recreate a section of your own garden. Take a look around outside for plants and tiny flowers to use to decorate your plate garden. Make fences from ice-cream sticks or twigs and use your imagination to help you create miniature copies of real-life objects. Use tiny pebbles to make a garden path. See if you can find some miniature ornaments that will be the right scale for garden statues.

You will need:

Plate

Sand

Potting compost

Pebbles

Sticks and thread

Dried flowers and moss

Selection of leaves and flowers

Modeling clay

Salt

Scissors

Paper

1 Place a layer of sand on a plate and cover it with a layer of potting compost. Use small pebbles to lay a path. Make some beanpoles from twigs tied with thread and press them firmly into the earth. Use some moss to create a hedge.

2 The garden is now ready for the vegetables to be "planted." A small-leaved plant stem has been wound round the beanpoles, and a slightly larger leaved plant stem is laid on the earth. The carrot leaves are made from maidenhair fern with clay models of vegetables and garden tools laid among the leaves.

3 The washing is drying in a corner of this sweet little flower garden. Begin with a layer of sand on a plate and cover that with a thin layer of potting compost. Use some checked paper to make the path and two long twigs tied with a piece of string to make the washing line. A piece of paper is cut to make the white picket fence. Now cut some paper clothes to hang on the line.

4 The washing is hung on the line and the garden in now full of flowers and plants. Use moss as plants and some dried flowers pressed into the earth.

5 This winter scene is very effective. Place a layer of sand on the plate and make a snowman from modeling clay. Plant a few moss bushes and press some twigs into the sand. When your model is arranged pour salt over everything to create a snow scene.

RECYCLED MILK CARTONS
Bird Feeders

Whether you live in the town or the country there will be wild birds about. You can easily attract the birds to your garden or windowsill by placing some wild bird seed in a small bird feeder where cats cannot get to it. The birds will enjoy a good meal and you will learn to recognize the different species. The bird feeder is made from an empty milk carton. If you hang it near a window you can keep an eye on the birds while you are out of sight, indoors. You might also want to thread some peanuts on a string and hang them out for the birds.

You will need:

Empty milk or juice carton

Scissors

Paint and paintbrush

Strong tape

String

Wild bird seed

Lard

Stale bread

Chopped apple and carrot

Small bowl

Saucepan

Spoon

1 Making this bird feeder is a good way to recycle a milk or juice carton. Cut away most of the sides of the carton leaving space at the base to hold the bird seed.

2 Once you have got the shape of the bird feeder right you can paint it. Choose a color that will blend in with the surroundings and not frighten off the birds.

5 To make a bird seed ball you will need a saucepan and some lard, available from a supermarket. Melt the lard in a saucepan over a low heat (you may need an adult to help you with this). Collect the rest of your ingredients together. You can use old bread and wild bird seed and could always add some chopped carrot, assorted nuts, or apple to the mixture.

3 When the paint is dry you can decorate the bird feeder. Attach a piece of strong tape in a loop to the top of the feeder and fill the base with some wild bird seed.

4 Hang your bird feeder in a place, safe from the reach of cats. Thread some peanuts on a piece of string and hang that up alongside the feeder.

6 Break a slice of bread into small pieces and place them in a bowl; pour over the melted lard. Add the wild bird seed and mix well together. As the mixture cools you will be able to form it into a ball. Push a piece of string into the center of the mixture. Once it has hardened you will be able to hang the ball up with the string, alongside your bird feeder.

Pressed Flowers

Flower pressing was a popular activity among ladies in the nineteenth century. Nowadays flower pressing is regaining popularity as a hobby. If you have a garden it is easy to find flowers to press, although you should check with an adult before you pick any flowers. Pressing flowers dries them out, flattening them and leaving a little of the original color. This creates a material you can use to decorate writing paper and greeting cards, and if you press enough flowers you could create a whole picture or cover a small box. Once you have pressed your flowers, store them flat between layers of tissue paper in a box in a dry, airy place to save their color.

You will need:

Fresh picked flowers to press

Flower press or old book

Scissors

Glue

Items to decorate

When picking flowers to press, make sure that they have no insects in them, and that the petals are perfect, not torn or brown.

Put the flowers in your flowerpress or in tissue between the pages of a thick book, as soon after picking as possible.

1 Pressing flowers is a wonderful hobby. Press the flowers flat in a flowerpress or use an old book. The flowers will need to be left in place for quite a few weeks before they are ready to use.

2 Pressed flowers can be used to decorate greeting cards. You can buy prepared cards to decorate or make your own from nice paper. Spend a little time trying out designs by laying different pressed flowers and leaves on the paper. When you are happy with your design use a little glue to attach the pressed flowers to the card. You may want to paint on a little varnish to give the picture a high gloss finish.

3 For a rose picture, press a whole rose carefully in your flowerpress. Leave it for a few weeks until most of the moisture has dried out. Choose a small frame and place the pressed rose in it. If you press lots of flowers you may have enough to cover a small box.

DRIED FLOWERS AND HERBS
Potpourri

To make your own potpourri you will first need to gather a selection of fragrant petals and dry them in a warm, airy spot away from direct sunlight. Roses and lavender are both very sweet smelling and can easily be grown in a town or country garden. A handful of rose petals can be dried in a paper bag hung up in an airy spot and small bunches of lavender flowers can be hung up on a line to dry naturally in the air. Once you have dried your petals you will be able to mix up some potpourri. You could place bowls of potpourri around a room to make it smell of summer or make some lacy bags to contain small quantities of potpourri to keep your drawers and clothes sweet smelling.

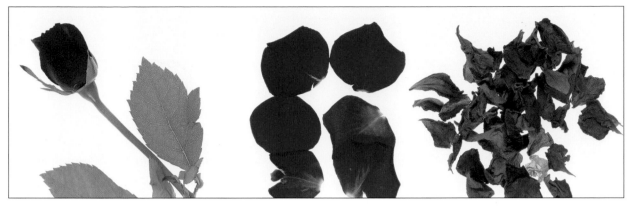

1 To dry rose petals you will need to place them in a warm airy spot away from direct sunlight. If you don't have the space to leave things out put a few petals in a paper bag and hang it up in an airy place. Choose some roses or other flowers which are sweet smelling. Check with an adult before you pick any flowers from the garden.

2 Besides petals you can dry orange and lemon peel, whole small flowers and some leaves. Spices can also be added to dried petals to enhance the perfume of the pot pourri. Cinnamon and mixed spice, cloves and nutmeg can all be put in pot pourri. If you don't have a flower garden to pick from, you may be able to purchase dried petals from your local wholefood shop. You could ask at the florist for any discarded flowers and buds.

3 One way of making good use of potpourri is to tie it in lace or muslin bags to place in your drawers and cupboards. They will make your clothes smell sweet and some petals and leaves will discourage moths and other unwanted insects from living among your clothes. When, after some weeks the scent fades, fill the bags with newly made potpourri.

Potpourri:

1 cup of fragrant dried rose petals and rosebuds

Half a cup of dried lavender petals

1 cinnamon stick, broken up

A large pinch of cloves

Dried orange peel, broken up

1 teaspoon of sea salt

Mix all the ingredients together in a bowl

You will need:

Dried rose petals and rosebuds

Dried lavender

Selection of dried fragrant leaves and petals

Bowl

Cinnamon sticks

Lace, muslin, and ribbon

Needle and thread

Leaf Pictures

In autumn the leaves on the trees turn from green to brown and all sorts of golden red colors in between. When you are out on an autumn walk collect some leaves of varying shapes, sizes, and colors. At home, press them between the pages of a book. Choose the colors carefully and make sure the leaves you choose don't have tears or holes. When they are dry they still show some of their color. You can then use them as bookmarks on their own and maybe save the best ones to frame as a picture, to hang on a wall, as a reminder of autumn. Try sponging the leaves with gold paint for a good effect.

1 To make a leaf picture choose leaves that have a good shape and color, and are not torn or broken. Carefully place them between the pages of a book and leave for several weeks to flatten and dry.

4 When the black paint is dry, give the leaves an antique metalic look by using a dry sponge with some gold paint. Don't cover the whole leaf with gold paint, make it patchy and interesting.

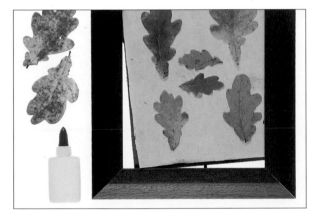 

2 When the leaves are ready, arrange them on a sheet of paper. When you are happy with the picture use glue to hold them in place. Put your picture into a frame.

5 When the gold paint is dry the leaves are ready to be placed in a frame. It may be an idea to collect a selection of leaves from a favorite walk. Press and gild them and when they are framed you can give the picture a title and sign it.

3 In this project the leaf pictures are made more decorative with gold paint, sponged over the leaves. Before you apply the gold, cover the leaves with a layer of black paint.

You will need:

Autumn leaves

Glue

Picture frame

Paintbrush

Black paint

Gold paint

Sponge

Saucer

Making Paper

Paper is made from recycled fibrous material—this could be newspaper, computer paper, sugar paper, mashed up potpourri, or leaves. You will need a small picture frame and an adult with a staple gun to help you make a paper making tray. The size of the picture frame will be the size of the sheet of paper you make, so bear that in mind when you choose your frame. Once you have mastered the art of paper-making you can experiment with colors and textures. Try laying pressed flowers on the wet sheet of formed paper or using different colored material. Food coloring can be used to color paper to good effect.

You will need:

Staple gun

Fabric

Wooden picture frame

Torn up pieces of
sugar paper

Kitchen blender

Container

Newspaper

Kitchen cloths

Rolling pin

1 To make a paper-making frame ask an adult to staple a piece of fabric taut over the back of a wooden picture frame.

2 Tear the paper up into small pieces and place it in the blender. Cover well with water. Blend until the paper is well mashed. Ask an adult for help with the electric blender.

3 Pour the well watered down paper pulp into a container large enough to take the paper-making frame. You will need enough pulp to half fill the container.

4 Lower the frame into the pulpy water and swish it around getting a layer of paper pulp into the frame. You may need to do this a few times to get the pulp evenly spread across the frame.

5 Lift the frame out of the water. Cover the work surface with old newspaper and lay a kitchen cloth on top of it.

6 In one movement tip the pulp out of the frame. You may need to give the frame a knock to get the pulp out. Place another kitchen cloth on top of the paper and press it down firmly.

7 Press evenly and firmly down on the kitchen cloth using a rolling pin. This will remove the excess water. You have now made a sheet of paper.

8 In this picture there are two sheets of hand-made paper. You will need to practice to get the amounts of pulp right and learn how to spread the pulp evenly across the frame.

OAK-GALLS, FRUITS, AND PETALS
Making Ink

People have been making ink since they could draw and write. Some of the oldest books in existence were written with ink made with oak-galls—try making some for yourself. Oak-galls are the swellings caused by gall wasp larvae burrowing into leaf buds. They are found on oak trees in autumn. Give them a good shake to ensure the insects have hatched and left home. You can also use colored fruit juice as ink—cranberries, raspberries, and cherries all stain in shades of red, while daffodil petals make a yellow ink. If you wanted to be secretive, try writing a letter in lemon juice. Once the writing has dried, you can bring up the message by ironing the paper with a warm iron. The message will color brown and you will be able to read it.

You will need:
Oak-galls, soft fruit, or petals

Pestle and mortar

Jar

Water

Rusty nail

Piece of muslin

Lemon

Paper and pen

1 You will need to find some oak-galls to make this ink. Pick them in the autumn after the insects have flown. Two or three oak-galls will make a couple of tablespoons of ink. Put the oak-galls in a mortar and crush them using a pestle.

2 Place the crushed oak-galls in a jar and add a tablespoon of water for each one and one rusty nail. Leave the mixture to stand, uncovered. After an hour you will notice that the liquid begins to change color. By the next day it should be quite dark and in a week it should be nearly black. Strain the ink through a piece of muslin and it is ready to use.

3 You can use dark colored fruit juice as ink. Use a dipping pen to write with. Cranberries, raspberries, and cherries will give shades of red and you can make a yellow from daffodil petals. Try different vegetables—beet gives a good color.

4 To make invisible ink you can use lemon juice. Squeeze the juice of half a lemon into a small container. Use a dipping pen or a thin paintbrush. Write your message on a sheet of paper and leave it to dry. To make the writing visible you will need to iron it, the writing will turn a brown color with the heat from the iron. Ask an adult for help with the iron.

Crunchy Salads

Sprouted seeds make good salads. They are crunchy to eat and packed full of vitamins. You could set up a small sprout farm on the kitchen windowsill and provide the family with fresh salad ingredients all through the winter months. Alfalfa seeds are small and tasty while mung bean seeds are larger. You can sprout sunflower seeds to make large and crunchy sprouts. Ask at your local health food shop for a list of suitable seeds for sprouting.

You will need:

Small piece of muslin

Saucer to draw around

Pen and scissors

Glass jar

Rubber band

Seeds for sprouting

Water

1 To sprout seeds you will need a jar with a muslin lid (so that the seeds can be washed and drained without losing any down the sink). You will need a piece of muslin and a large saucer; use the saucer to mark out a circle on the muslin.

3 Place one large spoonful of suitable seed in the glass jar (we have used mung beans). Cover the seeds with water and leave them to soak for two hours.

2 Cut away the excess fabric. This will be the lid of the glass jar. You will need a rubber band to hold the fabric onto the jar. You are now ready to start sprouting seeds.

4 Lay the muslin over the jar and hold it in place with a rubber band. You will need to rinse away the water. Wash the sprouts with water three times a day and watch them grow. When the sprouts are long enough to eat and before the leaves appear, take them out of the jar. Give them a good wash in clean water and use them in salads for a crunchy fresh taste.

Purchase seeds for sprouting from your local health food shop. Do not sprout seeds purchased for growing in the garden, they sometimes have chemicals on them to prevent pests eating them and can be harmful to people as well.

Twig Furniture

Rustic miniature furniture can be made from twigs and sticks found in the garden. You will need a sturdy pair of scissors and good strong glue for this. A set of miniature garden furniture could be useful when decorating a plate garden, or to sit outside a dollhouse. If you have a miniature teddy bear or doll use it to gauge how large the furniture should be. The early American settlers made real furniture for their cabins from roughly hewn wood. You could make a model cabin and decorate it with rustic furniture and found items from the garden.

You will need:

Sticks and twigs

Kitchen scissors

Glue

Some fabric for cushions or blankets

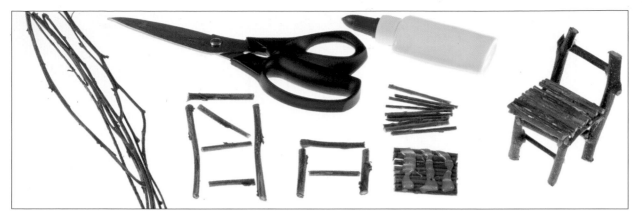

1 To make the chair you will need some sturdy twigs for the legs and back, and thin twigs to make the seat. It is a good idea to lay the sticks out flat and check their shape. Check that the cut pieces fit together as you go along. When you are happy with the shape of your chair use strong glue to stick it together.

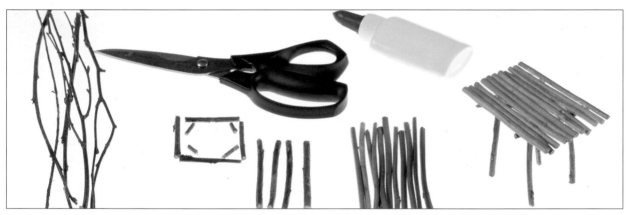

2 For the table choose four good straight twigs to use as legs. Make a frame and glue one leg to each corner. Make the top by laying the pieces down on the work surface and pour a line of strong glue on each end of the tabletop. Leave it to dry. When the frame and the table top have dried you can assemble your table.

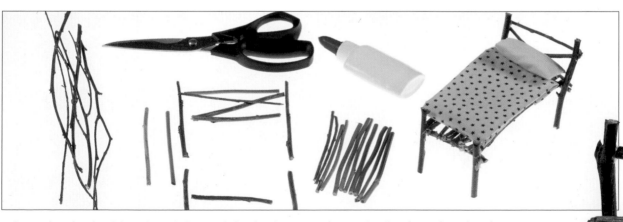

3 Make the bed head and foot of the bed first. The bed head is made by making a glued frame with diagonal pieces set in. The foot of the bed is the shape of a letter "H." When the glue has set, fix long twigs between the two ends. Use some fabric to make a mattress and quilt to cover the bed.

Desert Gardens

Growing a desert garden can be most rewarding. Garden centers and florists stock cactus plants. It is a good idea to check what plants are available before you buy a suitable planter. You will need a sunny windowsill on which to place your planted desert garden. Choose a pot large enough to hold a few cacti so that the overall impression is of a small corner of the desert. When you have planted the cacti, decorate the scene with some stones to resemble boulders.

You will need:

Flower pot

Gravel

Old spoon or small garden trowel

Cactus potting compost

Cactus plants

Suitable gloves

Selection of stones and crytals

White sand

1 Begin by placing a layer of gravel. This will provide drainage for the plants.

2 Next add a good layer of suitable cactus potting compost. Press it down firmly.

3 Dig small holes in the compost and plant the cacti. Remember to wear gloves.

4 Create a realistic-looking desert scene with some attractive stones and crystals.

5 When you are happy with the look of your desert garden, cover the compost with a layer of white sand. This will give the impression of desert sand.

Cactus plants need special growing conditions. Keep them hot in summer; place the desert garden on a windowsill that gets sunlight most of the day. Water your plants sparingly and regularly.

Always wear thick gloves when handling cacti as the spines and prickles are sharp.

DRIED LAVENDER, MOSS, AND ROSES
Dried Flowers

Drying flowers is a great hobby. Pick the flowers in summer and hang them up in an warm, dry, and airy place. To prepare them for drying, remove any leaves on the stem and tie them into small bunches or they will dry unevenly. It will take up to three weeks for them to dry. You can use them in a vase or create permanent arrangements of flowers in interesting containers. Dried flowers can also be used to decorate picture frames or make table settings for special occasions.

You will need:

Florist's foam

Knife

Terra-cotta pot

A selection of dried flowers

Glue

Scissors

A picture frame

1 Cut the florist's foam to fit. Place it in the flowerpot and press it down well.

2 Place a row of dried lavender bunches around the edge of the pot, pressing them into the foam.

3 Glue an edging of dried moss around the lavender on the edge of the pot. Using scissors, trim off any long or uneven pieces of moss.

4 Use a little glue and place some dried flowers and a dried rose in the center.

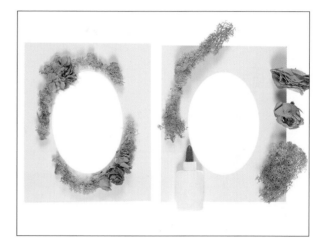

5 To make this dried flower picture frame you will need a cardboard frame, some dried moss and rosebuds. Begin by gluing the moss around the edge of the oval cut-out. Glue on the rosebuds and leave to dry. A picture frame would make an attractive gift. Offer it with a picture of you in the frame!

Bottle Gardens

Create a miniature oasis in a bottle. All you need to start a bottle garden is a large, empty candy jar and some potting compost. Choose plants which will stay quite small; ask for assistance at your local garden center or florist. Some garden centers have bottle garden departments where they sell small plants suitable for this enclosed, small environment. Bottle gardens should never have the sun shining directly onto them (they would get too hot), but they do need to be in a light situation. Keep the soil moist. You may not need to water often if the lid is kept firmly on. Feed your bottle garden every two weeks during the summer. Decorate it using glass paints and outliners. Choose a gold outliner for a stylish pattern or use black outliner and colored paint to create a stained glass effect on the exterior of the bottle.

You will need:

Sticks

Old spoon

Wire

Kitchen sponge

Cotton wool

A large empty candy jar

Pebbles or gravel

Suitable potting compost

Suitable plants

Glass paints outliner

Glass paint

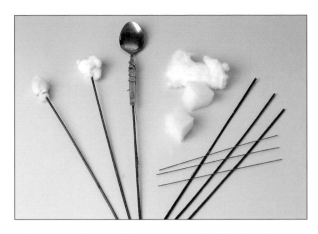

4 Use the digging tool to place individual plants in position. Press the compost down firmly around the plants, taking care not to damage their roots.

1 Begin by making some suitable bottle garden tools. For a digging tool, use an old spoon attached with wire to a long stick. Use a piece of kitchen sponge wired onto a stick to press the earth down when you are planting. Lastly, you will need a cleaning tool. For this use a piece of cotton wool wired onto a stick (you may need a few of these to tidy up the bottle garden once it is planted).

5 Use the cotton wool tool to clean up the sides of the bottle garden. Wipe away any smears or pieces of compost that have stuck to the sides of the jar.

2 Place a thin layer of pebbles or gravel in the base of the bottle. This will provide drainage for the bottle garden plants.

6 Your bottle garden is now ready to decorate. Choose a simple pattern and mark it out with the outliner. The stained glass effect will resemble a mini-conservatory.

3 Cover the pebbles with a thick layer of potting compost. Press the compost down gently using your sponge tool.

When choosing plants for your bottle garden choose low-growing varieties. Keep the compost moist but do not overwater. Feed your bottle garden every two weeks in the growing season.

Fragrant Wall Plaque

Keep your room sweet smelling with a fragrant wall plaque. Made from salt and flour dough the shapes are cut using cookie cutters. Add a few drops of essential oil to give them a nice aromatic smell. Hang your plaques on the bedroom wall or in a closet and they will smell sweet for a few months. You can always add more drops of oil when the perfume fades.

1 To make the salt and flour dough place the flour, salt, and water in a large bowl. Stir the mixture with a wooden spoon until it forms a dough. Remove from the bowl and knead for 5 minutes. When smooth, roll out the dough on a floured surface and cut out shapes with the cookie cutters. Place them on a greased baking sheet. Use the end of a straw to poke a hole in each shape (this is where the ribbon hanger threads through later). Bake the shapes in the oven at 265°F, for 4 hours or until completely dry.

2 When the shapes are dry and cool they are ready for painting on both sides. Leave a half-inch square area unpainted. This is where you put 2 or 3 drops of the essential oil to give the plaque its fragrance. When the paint is dry push a length of ribbon through the hole. Knot the ribbon and hang the plaque in the wardrobe or on the wall.

You will need:

2 cups flour
1 cup salt
1 cup of water
Large bowl
Wooden spoon
Rolling pin
A little spare flour
Cookie cutters
Baking tray
Paint
Paintbrush
Acrylic paint
Straw
Sweet smelling essential oil
(such as Lavender or Neroli)

In the Kitchen

Plant Pots

Don't throw away those empty yogurt cartons and margarine tubs; recycle them into these stylish plant pots. Create a set of matching planters for the kitchen windowsill using bright, eyecatching colors and white dots and plant useful herbs in them. A design of white hearts or flowers would look good in the bedroom with a leafy, green plant in it, or you could follow the step-by-step instructions and paint a green planter decorated with leaves and flowers.

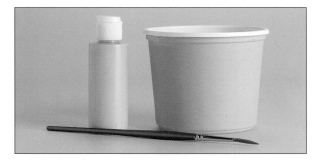

1 Paint on the base coat. Be sure to cover the pot completely. When it is dry check that the paint is even. You may need two coats to cover the pot well.

2 Paint a thin border at the base of the pot, then paint the rim. When this is dry, paint on the leaves in the same color.

3 Practice painting the flowers on a sheet of rough paper before you paint them on your pot.

4 When flowers are completely dry, paint on the white and yellow centres.

5 These yellow yogurt cartons don't need much decorating. Paint them in bright colors to grow cress in or use them for small plants.

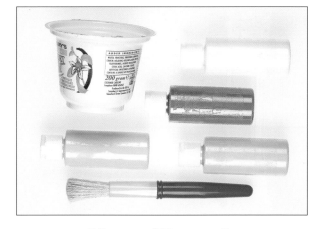

You will need:

A selection of recycled pots and tubs

Acrylic paint in a variety of colors

Paintbrushes

Paper towel or a cloth in case of spills

Acrylic paint will not stick to the tubs and pots unless they are spotlessly clean. Wash all your recycled pots in warm soapy water and rinse them well before drying them with a clean cloth.

Cover your work surface with newspaper before you begin painting.

VEGETABLES, MEAT, AND FISH
Burgers

Follow our easy recipes for burgers that are quick to prepare and delicious to eat. Make them from ground meat, cooked beans, tofu, or fish. There is a recipe to suit every taste. For a professional look, serve your burgers with a garnish such as a slice of lemon, cress, or sliced tomato and lettuce.

You will need:

Ingredients

Bowl

Potato masher

Wooden spoon

Frying pan

Plates and cutlery to serve

Bean Burgers:

1 can of black-eyed beans

1 small chopped onion, fried

1 teaspoon mixed herbs

1 egg

1 cup of brown breadcrumbs

Flour to roll the finished burgers in

A little oil for frying

Tofu Burgers:

8 oz. block of tofu, chopped

1 small chopped onion, fried

2 teaspoons fresh or dried parsley

1 cup brown breadcrumbs

2 teaspoons soy sauce

Sesame seeds to roll finished burgers in

A little oil for frying

Fish burgers:

8 oz. can of red salmon

1 cup brown breadcrumbs

1 small chopped onion, fried

1 teaspoon mixed herbs

1 egg

Flour to roll the finished burgers in

A little oil for frying

Beef burgers:

8 oz. ground beef

1 teaspoon mixed herbs

salt and pepper to taste

1 egg

half a cup of wholemeal breadcrumbs

Flour to roll the finished burgers in

A little oil for frying

1 Empty the beans or other main ingredient into the bowl and mash them well.

2 Add the rest of the ingredients and mix well with a wooden spoon. Use your hands to shape the mixture into burger shapes and roll in flour.

3 Fry in a little hot oil, serve on a burger bun. A tasty meal, easily prepared.

Always have an adult in the kitchen when you are cooking on top of the stove.

Wash your hands before preparing food.

FOIL Frames

Frame a special photograph in one of these pretty frames. They are made out of cardboard from a grocery box and covered with aluminum foil. Choose a simple shape and expect a few discards while you master the method. Simple patterns are best to decorate the frames: flowers, hearts, or stars, for example. Have a look around the kitchen and you may find colored foil you could recycle. The gold foil frame is made with recycled margarine tub foil! Try sprucing up an old picture frame by covering it with foil.

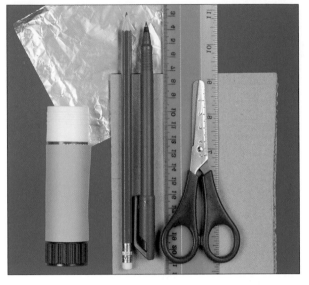

You will need:

Thick cardboard (from a grocery box)

Ruler

Strong scissors

Foil

Glue

Pencil and ballpoint pen

Remember foil is made from metal and can be sharp—take care.

1 Use a photograph to measure how large the frame should be. Cut out the foil shape an inch larger than the cardboard frame.

2 Spread the cardboard frame with glue and making sure there is no glue on your fingers, gently press the foil over the frame. Tuck the edges in well, smoothing the foil carefully.

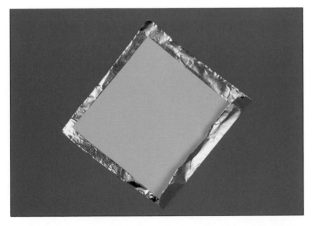

3 Cover the backing of the frame with foil.

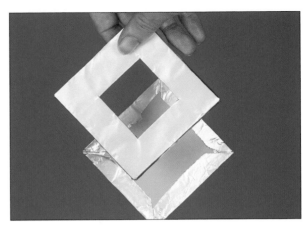

4 Attach the frame to the backing with glue on three sides, leaving an opening to slip in the photograph.

5 Use the ballpoint pen to mark the design onto the frame.

PEPPERMINT AND CHOCOLATE
Candy

Homemade candy is fun to make and delicious to eat! Try your hand at chocolate-dipped peppermints or cherries. The fruit is made from marzipan and painted with food coloring. You may find that making them takes a little practice, but once you have mastered the art you could make a bowl of miniature marzipan fruit. Have a look at some real fruit for inspiration. Fresh fruit can also be dipped into chocolate—try it with some orange segments.

You will need:

12 tablespoons of icing sugar

1 egg-white

Peppermint flavoring

Green food coloring

Wooden spoon

Bowl

Knife and board

Plain chocolate

Small bowl

Foil

Tray

Glacé cherries

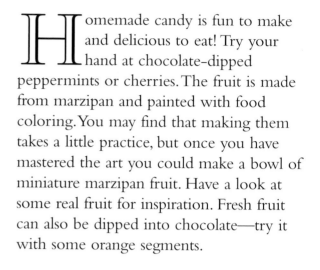

1 Place the icing sugar, egg-white, 4 drops peppermint flavoring, 12 drops green coloring into a bowl and mix well. You may need to add a little more icing sugar. Knead the mixture for a few minutes until it forms a smooth ball.

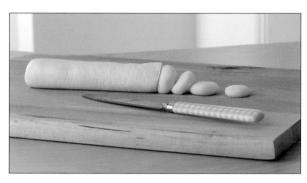

2 Form the mixture into a sausage shape and slice into disks. Use your hands to shape the disks into round candy shapes and place on a board to dry.

3 Ask an adult to melt the chocolate in a small bowl. Dip the dry peppermints into the melted chocolate until they are half covered. Place the chocolate dipped peppermints on a foil-covered tray to set.

4 To make chocolate-dipped cherries, first wash the syrup off the glacé cherries. Pat them dry with kitchen towel and use a cocktail stick to dip them into the melted chocolate. Decorate the dipped cherries with a small piece of cherry.

Always wash your hands before you handle food.

Remember to tidy up as you go along.

Egg Cups

Boiled eggs for breakfast will never be the same again with one of these fun egg cups. They are made from air-hardening clay. Make a Humpty Dumpty egg cup for a young brother or sister, or choose a more stylish crown or simple shape painted to match your breakfast plates. Make a set of egg cups, one for each member of the family, decorated to suit their hobbies or interests.

You will need:

A block of air hardening clay

Clay modeling tool

Tray to stand the egg cup on while it is drying

Acrylic paints

Paint-brush

Varnish

1 Begin by shaping a block of clay to be the wall for Humpty to sit on.

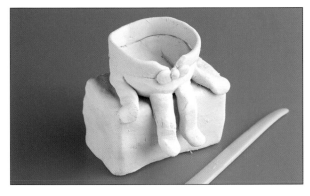

2 Make the legs and arms from sausage shapes and use an egg to gauge the size of the cup. Once you have made your model, leave it to dry for 24 hours.

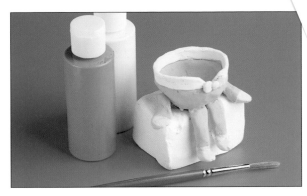

3 When the model is completely dry, you can decorate it. Paint one color at a time allowing each shade to dry.

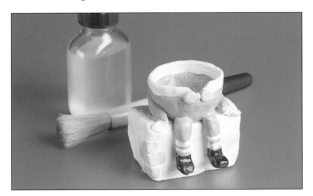

4 Varnish the egg cup when the paint is completely dry.

Before you begin, cover your work surface with newspaper or a plastic cloth—working with clay can be messy. It is a good idea to work on a tray which will enable you to carry your finished item to a safe place to dry.

If you cannot get hold of air hardening clay, make Humpty from salt and flour dough: mix 2 cups of flour and 1 cup of fine salt, add 1 cup of water and mix well. Knead for 5 minutes, then the dough will be ready for use.

SALT AND FLOUR
Dough Baskets

Use salt and flour dough to make a basket for bread rolls or fruit. Once baked in the oven the basket is ready for you to paint and varnish. Flower shapes or dough fruit make very good decoration. Use animal-shaped cookie cutters to make dough pets with the leftover dough. Always bake the pieces thoroughly and allow them to get quite cold before you paint them.

Salt and flour dough is not good to eat, so keep it away from young brothers and sisters.

Always wash out your paint and varnish brushes, to keep them clean and ready to use.

You will need:

Wooden spoon and large bowl

2 cups of flour

1 cup of salt

1 cup of water

A little spare flour

Rolling pin

Knife

Shallow oven-proof dish

Aluminum foil to line your dish

Acrylic paint and brushes

Water-based varnish

1 Use a wooden spoon to mix the flour, salt, and water well. When it forms a ball take it out of the bowl and knead it for 5 minutes. Sprinkle some flour onto the work surface to prevent the dough sticking as you work.

2 When the dough is smooth roll it out onto a floured surface and cut it into strips about an inch wide.

3 Cover a bowl with aluminum foil. Weave the strips into the bowl. Make the cherries from small balls of dough. Use a short piece of thin wire or two small sticks for the cherry stalks.

4 Bake the basket for 4 hours at 275°F, or until it is completely dry.

5 When your model is cool take it out of the bowl, paint and varnish.

Toast Racks

Brighten up the breakfast table with one of these easy-to-make toast racks. They are made from recycled grocery boxes and torn up strips of newspaper. Before you begin have a look around the kitchen and choose a color and style that will match.

Some toast racks have space for butter pats and jam while others only have room for toast. When you have made one of the simple shapes you could try something a little different. A nicely made toast rack would make a good gift for a friend or neighbor.

You will need:
Cardboard from a cardboard box

Sturdy scissors

Strong white glue

Water

Torn up pieces of newspaper

Acrylic paint and brushes

1 Use cardboard from a grocery box to cut out an oval-shaped base and four racks. You will need a pair of sturdy scissors.

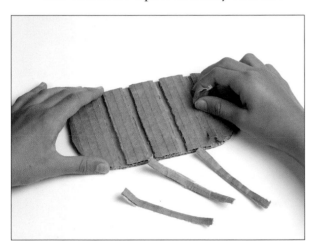

2 Use the blade of the scissors to score the card then tear out slots for the racks. Remember to leave enough space for the slices of toast between the racks.

3 Glue the racks into place and set aside until the glue has dried.

4 Mix an equal quantity of glue with water. Glue small torn pieces of newspaper all over your model.

5 When the toast rack is completely dry it is ready to decorate. Use acrylic paint and a design that matches the shape of your toast rack.

Remember to protect your work surface with newspaper or a vinyl cloth.

If you don't have any glue, get an adult to help you make some. Mix two cups of water and one cup of flour in a saucepan and cook it gently, stirring all the time, until it is thick, creamy, and sticky.

Fabric Printing

Decorate a traycloth or table napkins with apple or carrot prints. The prints are made using real fruit and vegetables cut in half. Green peppers make good prints too. Fabric paints come in plenty of colors and are easy to use—follow the directions written on the container. Always try your design out on a piece of scrap paper before you print on the fabric to test out how much fabric paint you need.

Protect your work surface with newspaper before you begin. Keep some kitchen towel handy in case of spills.

If you cannot get hold of fabric paint, try using acrylic paint. You will not be able to wash the cloth but it will make a great wall hanging for the kitchen.

You will need:

Vegetables

Knife

Sponge

Fabric paint

Squares of fabric

Cookie cutters

Kitchen towel

1 Cut a carrot in half. Use a sponge to spread a little fabric paint onto the carrot half. Gently press it down onto the fabric. Only press once and do not move it about when you press. Print a row of carrots on the cloth. Leave the printed cloth in a safe place to dry. Follow the directions that come with the fabric paint to set the dye.

2 Cut a potato in half. Press the cookie cutter firmly into the flesh of the potato. Use a knife to carefully cut away the excess potato. Remove the cookie cutter and you have a stamp ready for printing. Pat the stamp dry with some kitchen towel. Use a sponge to apply the fabric paint to the potato cut and print your pattern.

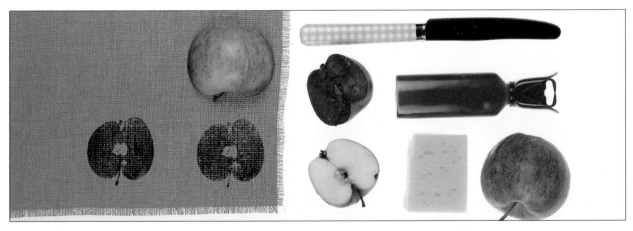

3 Halved apples printed on this green table mat look jolly. You will need to pat the cut surface dry with a piece of kitchen towel.

Use the sponge to apply red fabric paint to the apple surface and press firmly down onto the green table mats.

Glass Painting

Glass painting is a great hobby and a good way of recycling empty jars and bottles or personalizing glasses to give away as gifts or use in the home. Glass paints also work well on plastic containers, so collect a few large plastic containers and decorate them for use in the kitchen, for storing dried pasta or beans. Glass paints come in a wide variety of colors and are easy to use. Experiment with simple designs at first. Always try out your ideas on paper before painting on glass. If you make a mistake on the glass wipe the paint off quickly and start again.

1 Before you begin wash and dry the glass. Use the black outliner to mark up the pattern. Be sure there are no gaps for the glass paint to escape through. When the black outliner is completely dry use a dry brush to dip into the glass paint. Wash the brush well between colors and dry it before dipping it into the next color.

2 Use the gold outliner on its own for this stylish look. Think about what will be in the container when deciding on color and design.

3 Save tiny jars to decorate and fill with jam.

You will need:

Selection of glasses, jars, and bottles

Outliners in black, gold, and silver

Paintbrush

Water-soluble glass paints

Kitchen towel for spills

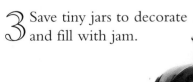

Remember to protect your work surface with newspaper before you begin.

Always make sure the glasses and jars are washed and dried with a clean cloth before you begin to decorate them.

Fridge Magnets

Liven up the fridge with a bright blue teapot or a friendly teddy bear fridge magnet. These fridge magnets are made from oven–bake clay, which comes in a wide range of colors.

Fruit and vegetable magnets look good in the kitchen, and a bright red apple, containing a friendly little worm, will bring a smile to everyone's face when at the fridge door.

Follow the manufacturer's directions when baking the clay.

Always have an adult present when using the oven.

1 Before you begin, make sure your hands are spotlessly clean as dirt transfers to the clay very quickly and can't be removed.

Knead the clay in your hand until it is soft enough to use. Shape the teapot following the steps in the picture.

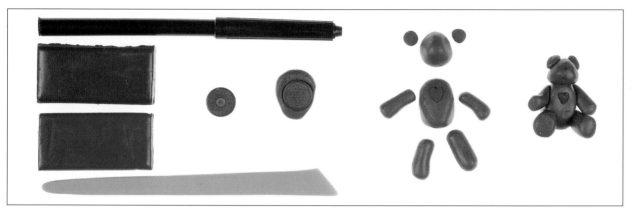

2 The bear is made from dark brown clay. Make his arms and legs from short sausage shapes. Give him a bright red nose, a bow tie, or even a colored hat! If the magnet doesn't stick, glue it on once your model is out of the oven and cooled down.

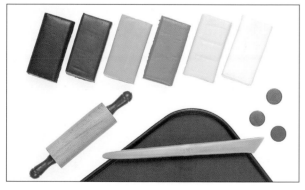

You will need:

Oven-bake clay in a variety of colors

Knife

Clean surface on which to roll your clay

Small rolling pin or a suitable pen lid

Baking tray covered with foil

Magnets

Glue

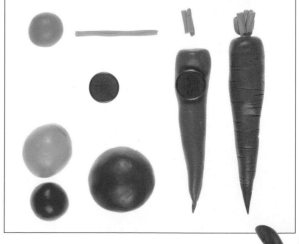

3 This carrot magnet is made from yellow and red clay mixed to give a good orange carroty color. Make the stalk from short rolls of green clay, squashed together.

ROLLS, TURNOVERS, AND PIES
Indoor Picnics

Rainy days are perfect for indoor picnics. Fill the hamper with egg rolls, cheese and potato turnovers, and delicious jam pies. Everyone will enjoy the turnovers which are easy to make and very filling. Use the leftover pastry to make a few jam pies. Simply cut out circles with a cookie cutter, place in a greased shallow muffin pan with a small spoonful of jam in each one. Bake for 12 minutes at 350°F. For the rolls filling, hard-boil an egg and when it is cool, chop it up and mix it with a small spoonful of mayonnaise. Spread it on rolls with some cress for a picnic treat.

You will need:

Bowl

Tablespoon

Rolling pin

Saucer

Knife

Baking tray

Fork

Pastry brush

Recipe for cheese & onion pasties

Pastry:

1 1/4 flour

1 stick margarine or butter

A little water

A little extra flour

Turnover filling:

1 cup of cooked diced potato

1 medium onion, chopped

3 oz. cheddar cheese, grated

Salt and pepper

1 egg, beaten

1 Make the pastry first. Place the flour and margarine (or butter) in a bowl, use your fingers to mix it until it looks like breadcrumbs. Add a tablespoon of water and mix well. You may need another tablespoon or two of water but add it a little at a time until the mixture is damp enough to make a ball.

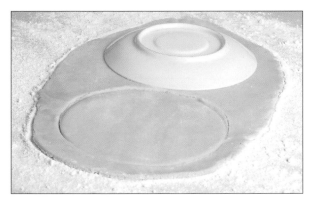

2 Sprinkle a little flour onto the work surface and roll the pastry out to a thickness of a quarter of an inch. Use a saucer to mark out the circles and cut them out with a knife.

3 Place the individual filling ingredients in a bowl. Mix them together well and add a sprinkling of salt and pepper.

4 Place the pastry circles on a greased baking tray. Place a large spoonful of filling in the middle of each pastry circle. Beat an egg in a bowl and brush a little on the edges of the pastry. Fold over the pastry to cover the filling. Use the fork to press down on the edges to seal the pastry parcel.

5 Use the pastry brush to paint egg over each finished turnover. Bake the turnovers for 25 minutes at 350°F.

Always check with an adult before you use the kitchen.

Ask an adult to help when using the oven.

Cookies

For a special treat, homemade cookies decorated with icing, silver balls cherries, and sprinkles, will brighten up your tea time. Try both recipes (plain and chocolate), cut out in a variety of shapes with a mixture of patterns and designs, to create a colorful plateful of delicious biscuits. A few homemade cookies in a decorative box or bag can make an ideal gift for parents or neighbors.

1 Use a wooden spoon to mix the flour, margarine (or butter), vanilla extract, sugar, and baking powder until it looks like breadcrumbs. Add the egg and mix with a wooden spoon until it forms a dough.

2 Sprinkle a little flour onto the work surface and roll out the dough with a rolling pin. Do not press too hard. Dip the cutters in flour before cutting out a selection of shapes.

3 Place the cookies on a greased baking tray. Bake for 15 minutes at 350°F. Allow to cool and decorate with icing, silver balls, cherries, and sprinkles.

Ingredients

1 1/4 cups plain flour

1 stick margarine or butter

1/3 cup castor sugar

1 teaspoon baking powder

1 egg

For plain cookies add:

1 teaspoon vanilla extract

For chocolate cookies add:

3 tablespoons cocoa powder

You will need:

Wooden spoon

Bowl

Cookie cutters

Cookie decorations

Ask an adult to help when using the oven.

MILK, YOGURT, AND FRUIT
Dairy Drinks

Mix up milkshakes and smoothies in moments using one of these quick and easy recipes. Turn the kitchen into a soda fountain and make drinks for the whole family. The smoothies are made from yogurt and fresh fruit, cooled down with creamy ice cream and the milkshakes are made from fresh milk, ice cream, and fruit. When you have tried these recipes maybe you would like to experiment with different flavors, fresh peaches and raspberry yogurt, or maybe a banana and fudge ice cream milkshake! Remember to decorate your drinks with slices of fruit, whipped cream and paper parasols. Serve with long spoons.

You will need
Blender

Fresh fruit

Selection of ice creams

Milk

Yogurt

Whipped cream

Straws

Decorations

Ask an adult to help when using the blender.

Strawberry milkshake

In the blender place 6 large strawberries, half a small banana, a scoop of strawberry ice cream, and half a glass of milk. Blend well. Serve with whipped cream and a coating of sprinkles on top.

Chocolate milkshake

In the blender place 1 small, roughly chopped banana, a large scoop of chocolate ice cream, and half a glass of milk. Blend well. Serve with whipped cream, two or three banana slices and chocolate sprinkles on top.

Banana smoothie

In the blender place 1 roughly chopped banana, a scoop of vanilla ice cream, and half a glass of natural yogurt. Blend well and serve in a long glass.

Strawberry smoothie

In the blender place 6 large strawberries, a large scoop of strawberry ice cream, and half a glass of strawberry yogurt. Blend well and serve in a tall glass with a blob of strawberry yoghurt and a strawberry on top.

ICE CREAM
Sundaes

Have an ice cream sundae party for your friends. You will need a selection of ice creams, fresh fruit, custard, cream, and decorative sprinkles. Try the home-made strawberry ice cream recipe, since it is quick and easy to make. Fruit yogurts can also be frozen and make tasty ice cream.

Always have an adult present when using sparklers or other fireworks.

Banana and chocolate ice cream sundae

Put one layer at a time into the glass. Start with some sliced banana, then add a spoonful of soft marshmallow. Sprinkle on some chocolate flakes, then a small scoop of vanilla ice cream and decorate with whipped cream.

Strawberry parfait

Begin with a layer of crushed graham crackers. Mix 2 teaspoons of strawberry jam with 2 teaspoons of warm water and pour over the crackers. Follow with soft marshmallow then some chopped strawberries and jelly. Finally decorate with whipped cream and a whole strawberry.

Sparkling ice cream sundae

Place a small tin of evaporated milk in the fridge for 2 hours. Pour the milk into a bowl and use a whisk to whip it until it is light and fluffy. Mix in the strawberries and syrup. Pour the mixture into a freezer-proof dish and freeze until solid. Serve it with a dazzling sparkler.

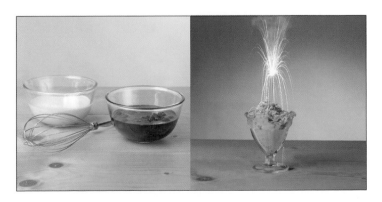

Miniature Teatime

Teatime in the dollhouse will go with a swing when you have made this tiny teaset and strawberry cream sponge. They are made from oven-hardening clay and baked in the oven. If you don't have any oven-hardening clay to hand you might want to use plasticene.

1 To make the miniature strawberry sponge cake begin with the plate. Use a flattened ball of red clay to make this. Next make two buff layers and two white layers and assemble the cake. Make some tiny strawberry shapes from red clay and place them carefully on top of the cake.

You will need:

Oven-hardening clay
White paint
Paintbrush
Baking tray
Yellow paper
Felt tip pen

2 Make the teapot and cups with matching saucers from red clay. Make a large ball of clay for the teapot. Make smaller balls for the teacups and press in your finger to form the cup shape. To make the handles and spout roll out thin sausage shapes and press them into position. Add a tiny ball of clay to make a teapot lid. To make the saucers flatten out balls of clay with your hand. Place the cake and crockery on a baking tray and bake according to the manufacturer's instructions. When the pieces are hardened, paint tiny white spots on the cups, saucers, and the teapot. Decorate a piece of yellow paper with felt-tip pens and lay out your miniature tea.

Indoor Crafts

Bookmarks

Bookmarks will always come in handy, whether you enjoy fairy tales or mysteries. These bookmarks are made from thin cardboard and colored with felt-tip pens. A bookmark made from your initial written in bubble writing and decorated with bright colors would take no time to make. You could take inspiration from the book you are reading or make one representing a particular hobby or interest.

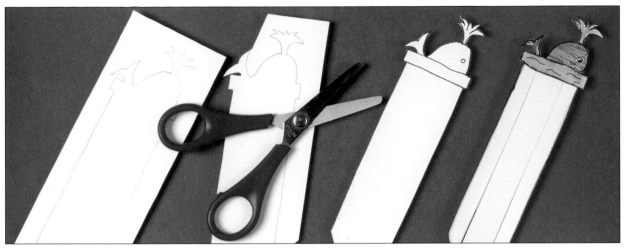

1 Use pencil to outline the whale. When you are happy with the shape cut it out.

Use felt-tip pens to color in the design and draw a neat border with a black felt-tip pen.

2 Personalize your bookmark by using your initial. Draw the outline in pencil first,

then go over it with a felt-tip pen before you decorate the inner part of the initial.

3 This bookmark would look good in a gardening book!

You will need:
Thin cardboard
Pencil
Scissors
Felt-tip pens

Paper Flowers

S urprise a friend with a bunch of scarlet poppies and fantasy flowers. They are made from tissue paper and florist's wire. The poppies are made up of individual petals and look quite realistic with their black-fringed stamens. The fantasy flowers are easy to make from layers of different colors. Let your imagination run riot and create a rainbow bouquet.

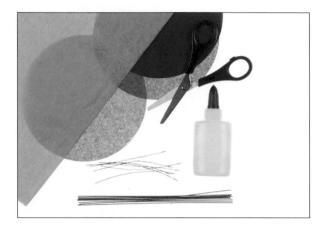

You will need:

Glue

Tissue paper in a variety of colors

Florist's wire

Green florist's tape

Scissors

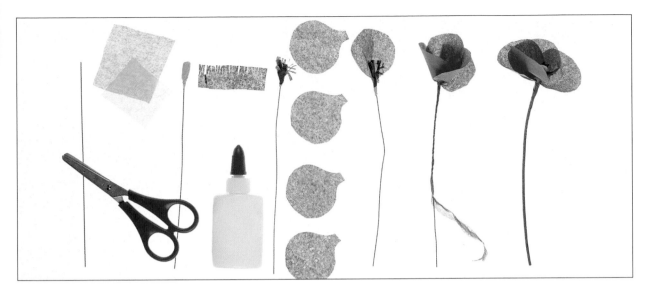

1 Glue a scrunched-up piece of tissue paper onto one end of a piece of wire, for the center of the poppy. Now glue the square of green paper over the poppy center. Roll the black-fringed piece around the center of the flower to make the stamens. Glue on the petals one at a time. Bend them slightly so they look realistic. Finally, use the green tape to tidy up the base of the flower and cover the wire.

2 Fantasy flowers are made from layers of colored flower shapes. Begin by cutting the shape for the base or sepals of the flower. Layer three colors of tissue paper together, cut out a flower shape, and then cut a small hole through the center of the papers. Wind a small piece of paper around a wire to make the flower center. Now use glue to attach the green sepal shape and the colored flowers. Finally use the green tape to tidy up the base of the flower and cover the wire.

Making paper flowers takes practice. Don't expect the first one to come out perfectly. Keep trying until you get a good shape make a bunch.

CARDBOARD AND PAPER
Teddy Bears

Make a whole family of cut-out bears and design outfits for them—playclothes, fancy dress, pajamas. These bears are drawn on thin, white cardboard and colored with pencil crayons. If you do not have any cardboard to hand, use cardboard from a cereal box to make the bears and their outfits. A simple folded bed would be fun to decorate.

You will need:
Thin cardboard or stiff paper

Pencil

Crayons

Scissors

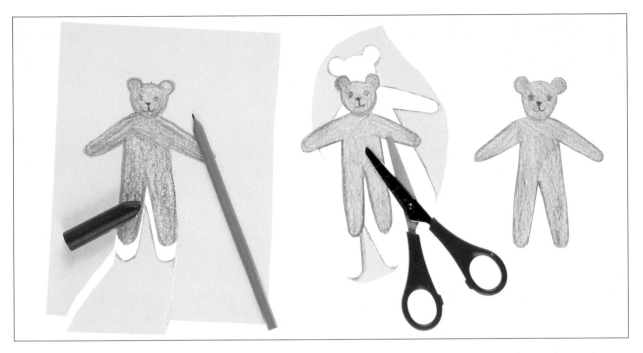

1 Draw a teddy bear onto thin cardboard. Give it a face and color it in using bright crayon colors. Cut it out. Make several members of a teddy bear family to dress.

2 Lay the cut-out teddy bears onto paper or thin cardboard and draw an outfit around each shape. Fill in and color.

Remember to tidy away all the scraps of paper and cardboard when you have made your cut-out bears.

FELT
Beads

Turn ethnic-looking beads made from colored felt into great chokers, bracelets, and pendants. The beads are made from layers of felt glued or tied together. They are threaded on embroidery silk. Make a selection of colors and shapes and combine them with wooden beads to make an exotic necklace.

You will need:

Felt squares (from a craft shop)

Scissors

Fabric glue

Rubber band

Needle and colored thread

Small quantity of stuffing

Ribbon

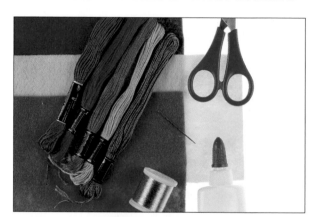

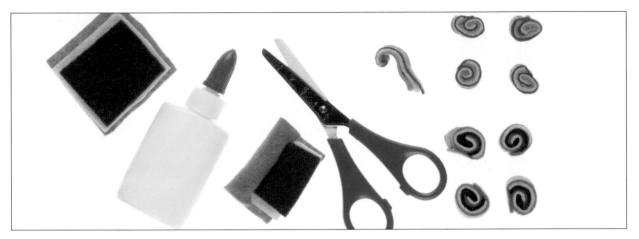

1 Cut three squares of colored felt, each slightly smaller than the other. Layer them, using a little glue to hold them in place. Now roll them tightly in a sausage shape and hold in place with glue. You may need to wind a little thread around them or hold them in place with a rubber band. The glue will need to dry thoroughly. When the glue has set, use scissors to cut the sausage into beads.

2 You will need two squares of colored felt. Cut out a heart shape from each color, with one heart slightly smaller than the other. Place a little stuffing between the layers and sew them together with colored thread. Make a ribbon loop at the top of the heart for threading.

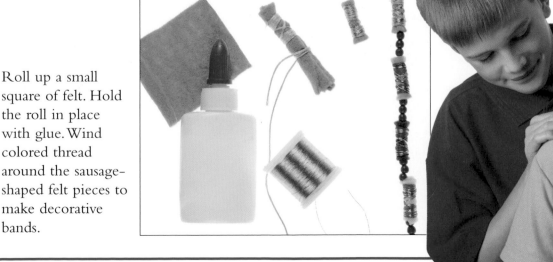

3 Roll up a small square of felt. Hold the roll in place with glue. Wind colored thread around the sausage-shaped felt pieces to make decorative bands.

Friendship Bracelets

Friendship bracelets are easier to make than you think; they just take a little time to practice. Choose several threads in strong or pastel color combinations. Find a corner to settle down on your own where you can work without interruption and in time you will master the art and make a braid to wear and one to give to a special friend.

You will need:

Cork board or work surface

Selection of colored thread

Sticky tape or safety pins

Scissors

1 You will need three lengths of thread. Make a knot to hold the threads together and attach the knot end to the board or work surface with tape or a safety pin.

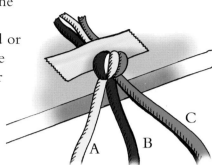

2 Hold thread B with your left hand; Take thread A around B and push it through the loop to make a knot and pull the thread.

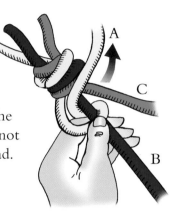

3 Repeat this action. You should have two knots on thread B.

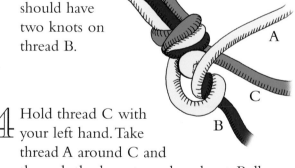

4 Hold thread C with your left hand. Take thread A around C and through the loop to make a knot. Pull the thread and then do it again. You should now have two knots on thread C. Thread A is now on the righthand side and you have completed the first row.

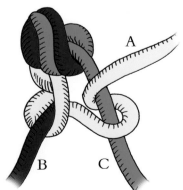

5 To start row two, make knots from left to right; knot B twice onto C, then twice onto A. For the third row, knot C twice onto A, then twice onto B.

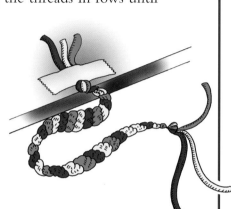

6 Keep knotting the threads in rows until you have made a braid long enough to go around your wrist. Tie a firm knot to hold the loose ends in place.

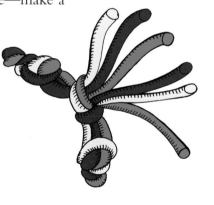

7 Your friendship bracelet is now complete—make a double knot at each end and trim away any excess thread.

Remember to protect your work surface with newspaper or a vinyl cloth.

To make a wider braid use four, five, or six threads. Make the braid as described above, knotting each thread twice, from left to right.

Brooches

Use oven-bake clay to make these cheeky brooches. Glitter-spangled stars, leaping dolphins, tiny toadstools, or a fat pink pig—these will all look great on a felt beret or a coat lapel. The glitter star is made from colored clay with the glitter glued on after baking. A coat of varnish gives a good finish.

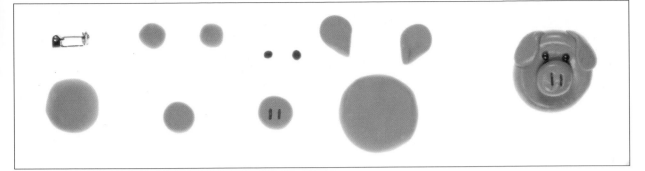

1 To make this pink pig brooch start with a disk of pink clay to make the face. The nose is made from a small cylinder shape. Use the modeling tool or a cocktail stick to mark nostrils on the nose. The ears are made from flattened tear drop shapes flapping over the face. Make two little black eyes and when all the parts are assembled, place your pig brooch on an oven tray, ready for baking.

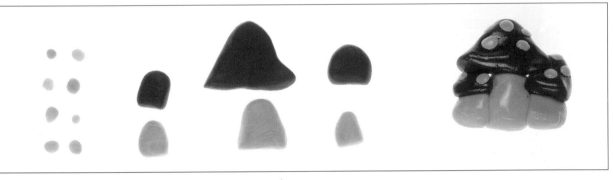

2 To make a cluster of toadstools, begin by making three stalks, one large and two small, out of yellow clay. Squash them gently together. Now make the caps from red clay and press them carefully onto the stalks. Decorate the caps with tiny yellow dots and your toadstool brooch is now ready for baking. After baking, when the clay has cooled, varnish the shapes. With an adult's help, glue on the brooch backs.

You will need:

Oven-bake clay in a variety of colors

Modeling tool

Oven tray

Varnish

Brooch backs

Suitable glue

When using oven-bake clay you will need to soften the clay first by molding it between your fingers.

Follow the manufacturer's directions when baking the clay.

Always have an adult present when using the oven.

Ask an adult for help when attaching the fastener to the brooch as you will need to use a strong glue.

CALICO
Candy Cushions

Dyed with wax crayons, these cushions will look soft and cuddly on your bed or on the playroom sofa. The cushions are made with calico fabric and are easy shapes to cut out and decorate. The wax crayon patterns can be ironed on to set them firmly. You could make a whole bag of candy cushions for your bed. A calico cat or doll would be great fun to decorate with wax crayons.

You will need:

Calico fabric

Wax crayons

Scissors

Needle and thread

Polyester stuffing

Brown paper

1 Fold the fabric in half to make a double layer. Draw on a large wrapped candy shape on the calico.

3 Cut out the cushion shapes and turn them right sides in. Sew together leaving a gap for the stuffing.

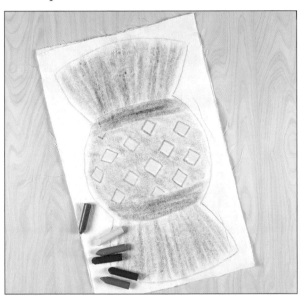

2 Use the wax crayons to color the candy shape in swirls and dots, making it as realistic as possible.

4 Turn right side out. At this stage you should ask an adult to help iron the cushion shape between brown paper to seal the dye. Stuff the cushion with polyester.

RECYCLED PLASTIC
Mobiles

Recycle milk and juice containers and turn them into colorful mobiles. The sleepy sheep would look good above your bed and the stars and flowers could hang in a sunny window. The mobiles are painted using water-soluble glass paints and outliners. If you don't have those to hand you can use colored, permanent markers instead to create a similar effect.

You will need:
Florist's wire
Small pliers
Flat sided plastic milk or drink carton
Scissors
Outliner
Paintbrushes
Water-soluble glass paints
Needle
Gold thread

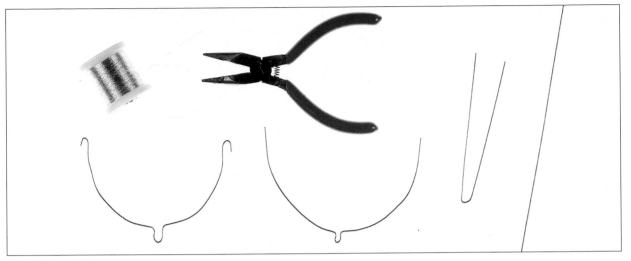

1 Florist's wire is easy to bend; start with an 8 in. length. Begin by folding it in half. Then use the pliers to shape the mobile hanger and hooks. You will need three hangers for each mobile and each hanger should be exactly the same shape and size.

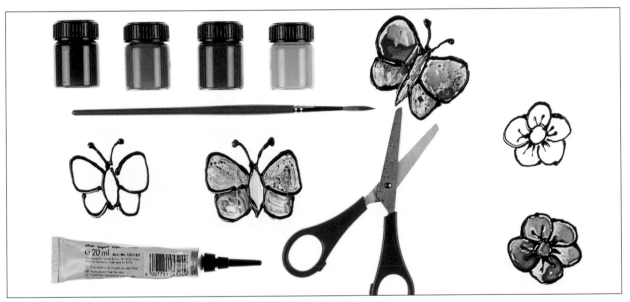

2 Use the scissors to cut the plastic container into suitable shapes for decoration. Wash the shapes and dry with a clean cloth. Outline the design and when the outliner is hard use a dry brush and glass paint to color the shape.

3 Assemble the mobile by making a hole with the needle through the shapes and threading the gold thread through. Hang up the shapes and your mobile is complete.

Letter Rack

Keep your mail in check with these bright red tulips! The letter rack is made by slotting together thick colored card shapes. Once you have mastered the technique you will be able to create your own designs, such as these flower patterns, or maybe have a go at the ship at sea. The ship is a little more detailed, with the design cut from colored paper.

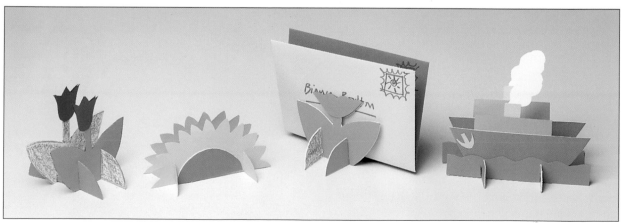

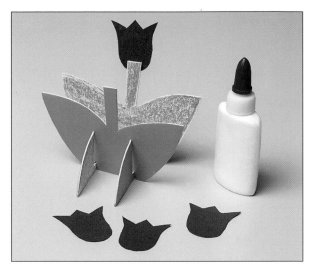

1 Draw the design on thick, colored cardboard. The green bases will need to be cut straight to stand level on the table. The flowerheads are cut from colored paper. Cut all the pieces out.

3 Glue on the flower heads and your letter rack is ready to hold the mail.

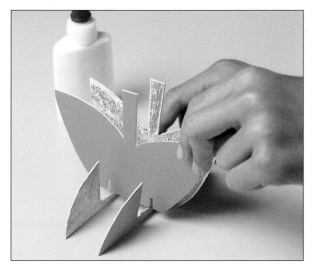

2 Color the plain side of the card with crayons. Slot the letter rack together. You may need to make a rough one first to get the shape and slots right.

The letter rack can be made of cardboard cut from a cereal or grocery box. You may need to cover the pieces of card with a layer of papier-mâché to make them more sturdy and create a good surface to paint or color.

You will need:

Thick colored cardboard

Scissors

Colored paper

Crayons

Glue

Thin colored cardboard

Mirror Painting

irror, mirror on the wall who is the fairest of us all? Paint one of these pretty designs on a mirror tile to put up on the bathroom wall. The tiles are painted with glass paint, which is available in a wide selection of colors and is very easy to use. The outliner divides the colors and comes in tubes that you use like a ballpoint pen, squeezing the color gently onto the mirror.

You will need:

Mirror tiles or handbag mirrors

Glass paint outliners

Paper towel to mop up spills

Paintbrushes

Water-soluble glass paints

1 Use the outliner as if it were a pen, squeezing gently to allow a steady stream of the thick liquid onto the glass. Keep your paper towels handy in case of spills.

2 When the outliner is completely hard you can paint in the color. Use a dry brush to dip into one color at a time and wash and dry the brush well between colors.

Wirework

Colored furry wire is a great craft material as it is easy to form into flowers, leaves, and other fancy shapes. Fill a small flower pot with wire flowers for a pretty gift, or make a bunch of red blooms to brighten up a dull corner. Glitter wire can be shaped into stars and hearts, and pressed into cork to make a romantic message.

You will need:

Colored furry wire

Glitter wire

Felt-tip pen

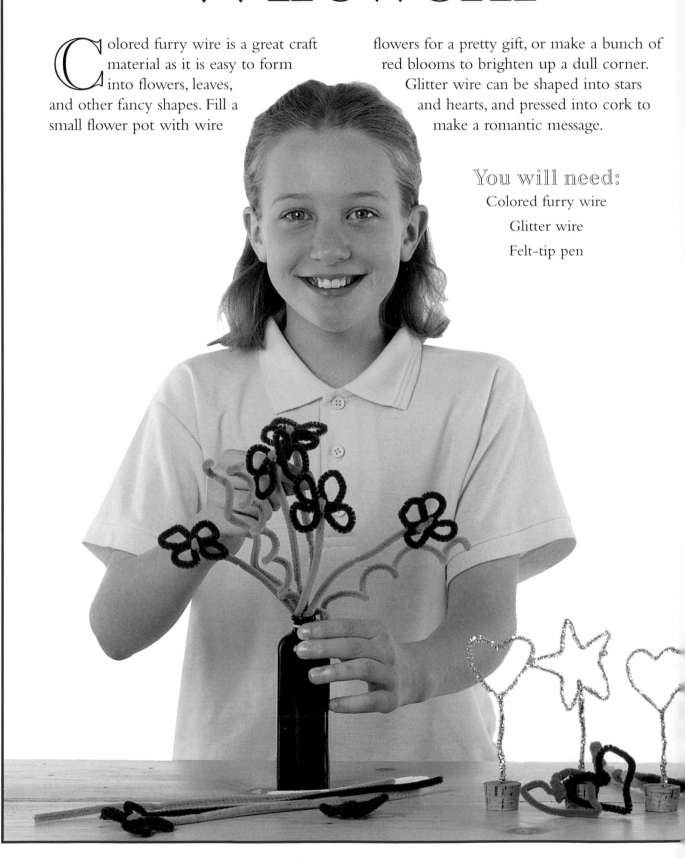

1 Bend the red wire into a flower shape. Wind the end of a piece of green wire around the centre of the flower—leave the long end to form the stalk.

Make the leaves by winding green wire around a felt-tip pen then easing it off. It will hold its shape. Put the flowers and leaves into a vase.

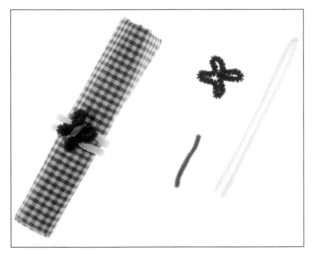

2 To make a napkin holder bend the white wire to form a circle. Decorate with a red wire flower. Fix it on with green wire.

3 Shape silver wires into these attractive table decorations. Push the shaped wire into cork to make a support or stand.

Bent furry wire can be straightened by pulling it between a finger and thumb a number times until it resumes its original shape.

Animal Pegs

Hold notes to your clipboard with a wild animal peg. The animals are drawn, cartoon-style, on thin cardboard and colored using felt-tip pens. You could try gluing one of the finished pegs onto a magnet and attaching it to the fridge to hold notes. Practice your drawing on scrap paper first and look at comic strips and story book illustrations to get the style right.

You will need:

Thin cardboard

Pencil

Scissors

Felt-tip pens

Eraser

Glue

Pegs

Have a good look at these examples before you begin. Draw an outline with pencil. When you are happy with the shape, color in the animal using felt-tip pens. If you draw a dark outline around the colored animal, you will see that this makes a big difference and gives the picture a professional finish. Cut out your animal and glue it onto a peg.

OVEN-BAKE CLAY
Miniature Farm

This miniature farm can be made in an afternoon and could provide endless pleasure for a younger brother or sister. Stand it on a sunny windowsill to create a pretty country scene. Make a storage box for the farm from a matchbox covered with colored paper and decorated in farmyard-style.

You will need:
Oven bake clay
Modelling tool and cocktail stick
Oven Tray
Match box
Colored paper
Scissors

1 Begin by softening the white clay. Make the body first, then flatten a strip and fold it over the body as the ears. Now soften a small piece of black clay, and roll it into a sausage shape. Use the modelling tool to cut the legs and face.

2 These colorful hens are made from a small ball of brown clay. Press the clay to shape the head and tail of the hen. Make a base from a ball of green clay. Pinch out tiny pieces of red and yellow clay for the beak and comb.

3 First soften the pink clay. Make a nice round sausage shape for the body. The pig's snout is made from a small flattened ball and its ears are made from flattened teardrop shapes. Roll out a smaller sausage shape and use the modelling tool to cut short legs. Roll out a thin tail and attach it firmly to the body.

To make some little patches of daisy-covered grass flatten an oval shape of green clay. Then make some small balls of yellow and green clay and use a cocktail stick or the tip of your modelling tool to lift them up and press them down onto the clay grass. When all your models are made, place them on a baking tray and harden them in the oven.

Follow the manufacturer's directions when baking the clay.

If you can't buy oven bake clay, you can use plasticine.

Scrunchies

Easy to make, you can have a scrunchy for every occasion. Sew them by hand in a running stitch or ask an adult to sew them for you, using a sewing machine. Thread them with elastic and decorate them imaginatively. Make scrunchies from ribbon, lace, velvet or dress fabric. A brightly colored towelling scrunchy would be good for the seaside or swimming pool.

You will need:
Fabric and lace

Needle and thread or a sewing machine

Medium-sized safety pin

One quarter inch wide elastic

Scissors

Sequins and glue

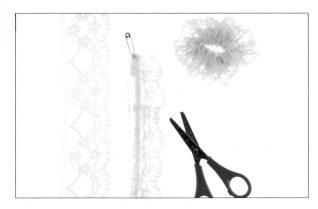

1 Lace: sew a one quarter inch wide hem along one edge of the lace. Use the safety pin to thread the elastic through the seam. Tie the ends of the elastic into a knot and shape the scrunchy.

3 Tartan: this attractive scrunchy is made in the same way as the velvet scrunchy. Use matching thread to sew the seams.

2 Velvet: fold the fabric in half lengthways, with the wrong side out. Sew a seam. Turn the velvet tube the right way round by pulling one end through the other. Sew a channel in matching thread along one side and thread the elastic through.

4 Sequin: make this party time scrunchy in the same way as the tartan and velvet scrunchies. Decorate it with shiny sequins glued or sewn onto the fabric.

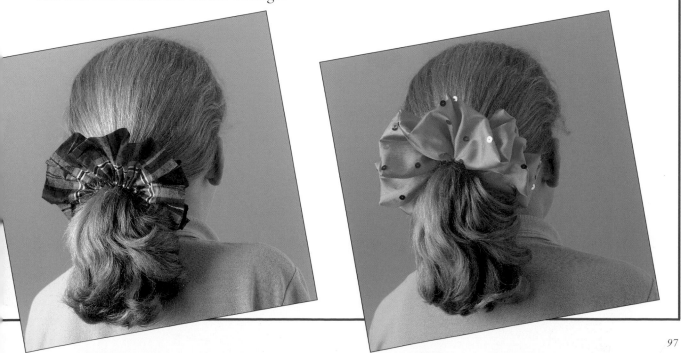

AIR-HARDENING CLAY
Brilliant Beads

Rolling beads from clay is a good rainy day craft. These beads are made from air-hardening clay and painted with bright colors. Use a fine paintbrush to paint on the tiny flowers or white spots. Maybe you could design a special pattern to go with a special outfit.

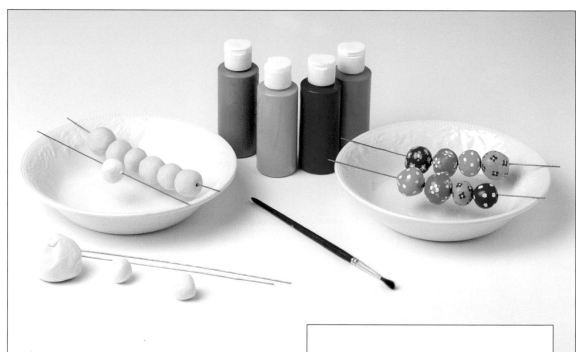

1 Make balls of clay in your chosen size (you might want to make small beads for a necklace or chunky beads for a bracelet). Push the wire through the middle of each ball wiggling it a bit to create a good sized hole. Lay the wired beads across the bowl and leave them in a dry airy spot to harden completely. Leave the beads on the wires while you paint and then varnish them. When you are happy with them, remove them from the wires and thread your home made beads as a necklace or bracelet.

You will need:
Air-hardening clay
Wire
Bowl or box to lie the wired beads
across while they dry
Paintbrush
Paint
Water soluble varnish
Thread

Cards and Wrappings

Sticker Fun

Decorating writing paper is a great way to make good use of a sticker collection. Stickers come in such a wide range of colors and styles, you could customize writing paper to suit almost every hobby or lifestyle. Choose brightly colored writing paper to decorate and find matching envelopes. Use a large sheet of paper to make a folder for holding your matching writing paper and envelopes. You will always be able to find them when you need to send a letter.

You will need:

Colored paper

A selection of stickers

1 Choose brightly colored writing paper to make good use of the stickers. These rainbow stickers look stylish centred at the top of the page.

2 Decorate the envelopes with a sticker on the bottom left-hand corner. You could coordinate your paper and envelopes using two colors.

3 To make a folder for your decorated paper, fold up a large sheet of thin cardboard, three quarters its length, leaving a piece to fold down into a flap.

4 Hold the sides together with colorful stickers and decorate the front of the folder with matching stickers.

Gift Boxes

Surprise your friends with one of these stylish handmade boxes. Make small boxes from paper or slightly larger boxes from thin card. A double layer of wrapping paper would make an attractive box. Use paper that suits the gift and make a box from flowery paper to hold packets of seeds or use red paper for a Valentine box. Plain paper can be decorated with stickers or colored tape. Try decorating paper first with crayons or pencils. A set of boxes could be used to hold cake and party favors and you could personalize the boxes with your guests' names. Once you have mastered the method you will find the boxes quick and easy to make.

You will need:

Paper

Ruler

Scissors

Glue

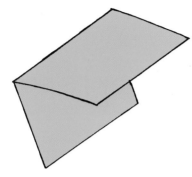

1 Fold a rectangular piece of paper in half.

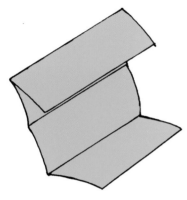

2 Fold each half in on itself, so that both ends meet in the middle.

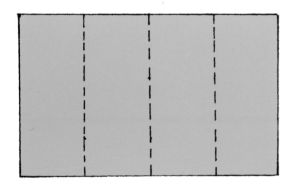

3 With the paper opened out, you will see crease marks like this.

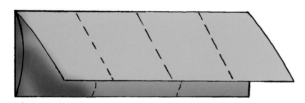

4 Now fold the paper into thirds in the opposite direction to your first folds.

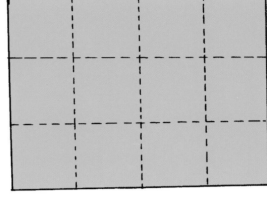

5 Now the creases should look like this.

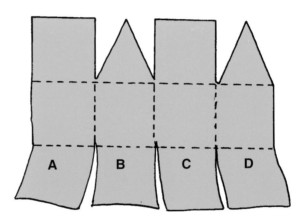

6 Cut along the crease lines and cut out the triangles as shown in the picture above.

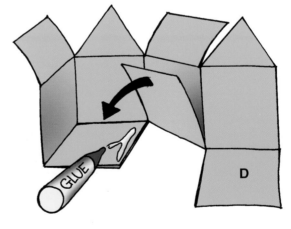

7 Fold in and glue flap B onto flap A, flap C onto flap B and flap D onto flap C. Finally stick the open edge with tape on the inside and make a hole at the top of both triangles for a ribbon.

THIN CARDBOARD AND PAPER
Pop-up Cards

This pop-up card is simple to make and will brighten up someone's day. When placed on a windowsill or mantlepiece it will look as if a bunch of flowers is bursting out of the card. The cards are made and decorated with thin cardboard. If you don't have any colored thin cardboard available, cut up a cereal box and paint it in bright colors yourself.

You will need:
Colored thin cardboard

Scissors

Glue

Coloured paper

Felt tips pens

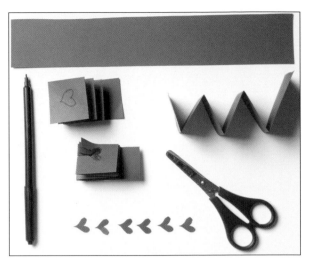

1 Begin by folding a sheet of thin cardboard in half and then open it out. Cut out a small square of cardboard and fold it in half. Fold a lip on the two edges, and glue these into the card to make the vase. Open and close the card to check that the vase flattens.

3 Cut small heart shapes to decorate the vase from red paper, folded over.

2 Using green thin cardboard, cut the stalks and leaves, use glue to attach these to the inside of the vase. Cut out some tulip-shaped flowers and glue them onto the stalks, making sure that they are hidden when the card is closed.

4 Now decorate the front of the card with a large red heart and a smaller blue heart, to match the rest of the design. Now you are ready to write your message on the card, using felt tip pens.

When trying out something for the first time, start by making a rough example out of scrap paper and cardboard.

Bows & Ribbons

Bows and ribbons provide the final touch to a beautifully wrapped gift. You can decorate plain ribbon with felt tip pens, creating your own designs. The ribbons shown here are decorated with tiny motor vehicles and balloons, but any design would be fun. Hallowe'en pumpkins or Christmas trees are bright and easy to draw. Bows are quick to make using the method shown. Choose thin ribbon to make small bows and wider ribbon for larger bows. Coordinate the patterns and colours of your homemade bows with wrapping paper for a stylish look.

You will need:

Ribbon

Felt-tip pens

Ruler

Scissors

Needle and thread

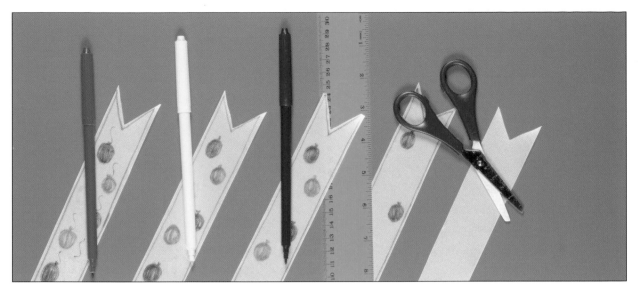

1 Use felt tip pens to decorate plain ribbon. Cut a little ribbon off to practice on. Press the pen down gently to prevent the color bleeding across the weave of the ribbon.

Complete the use of one color before moving on to the next. Remember to repeat your pattern to give the ribbon a store-bought look.

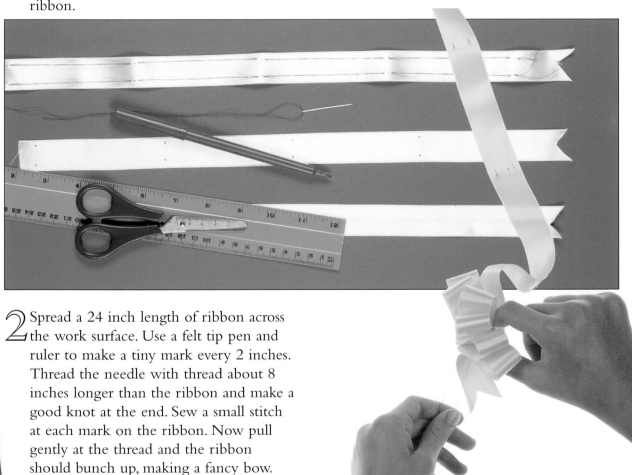

2 Spread a 24 inch length of ribbon across the work surface. Use a felt tip pen and ruler to make a tiny mark every 2 inches. Thread the needle with thread about 8 inches longer than the ribbon and make a good knot at the end. Sew a small stitch at each mark on the ribbon. Now pull gently at the thread and the ribbon should bunch up, making a fancy bow.

PAPER
Printed Cards

Spend a rainy afternoon making potato cuts to print with and you will be able to set up a production line and make a collection of cards or writing paper. The fish card is made with layers of different colored paper, each slightly smaller than the other. Cookie cutters come in lots of shapes and provide a quick way to make home made stamps. Use a small rabbit shape to decorate writing paper and envelopes. The bunch of carrots is made by first drawing the shape onto the potato half, then cutting it out with a knife. A set of cards tied with matching ribbon would make a good gift.

You will need:

A potato

Cookie cutters

Knife

Paint and saucer

Sponge

Paper

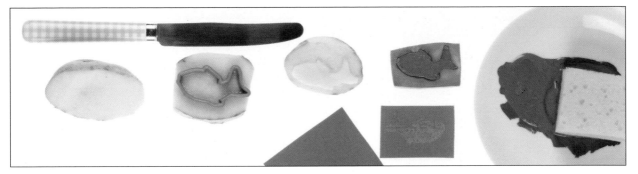

1 Begin by cutting a potato in half. Take the fish-shaped cookie cutter and press it firmly into the flesh of one half of the potato. Use the knife to cut around the shape. Lift off the cutter and remove the excess potato flesh. Put a little paint onto a saucer and use the sponge to evenly distribute the paint on the stamp. Now press the stamp gently onto blue paper. Print a few fish and leave them to dry.

2 Take a white sheet of paper and fold it in half to make the card. Now take a square of blue paper slightly smaller than the card and glue it on the front. Next glue on a small piece of gold paper. Cut out the fish print and glue it on top.

3 To finish off the picture you will need to make a simple stamp from the other half of the potato. Use the knife to cut a weed shape. Spread green paint on the stamp and print leaves of seaweed onto the card. Leave to dry.

Protect your work surface with newspaper or a plastic cloth before you begin.

It is a good idea to practice stamping your design on some scrap paper to get an idea of how much paint you need to apply to the stamp.

Concertina Cards

Make one of these cards and watch the concertina movement when you open and close the card. The clown gives a good impression of playing his concertina, and the ballerina's tutu stands proudly out. The poodle's ruff looks almost real! The cards are quite simple to make, so think up some ideas of your own. You could use the concertina shape to make a bumble bee's body, or maybe a wriggly worm holding an umbrella! Use a little imagination and some brightly coloured paper to create a novel concertina card for a friend's birthday.

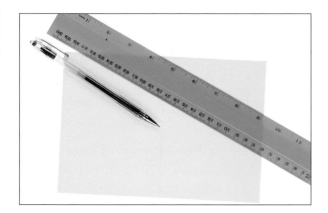

1 Fold a sheet of paper in half to form the card. Use the ruler to measure where to fix the concertina ends. Mark the two points, which should be evenly spaced on either side of the central fold.

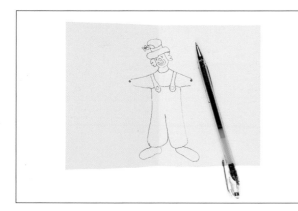

2 Draw the clown with the arms ending at the dots. Make the picture quite simple.

3 Color in your picture with bright shades, making it as attractive as possible.

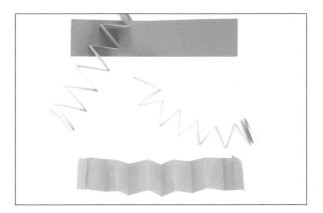

4 You will need to cut a long narrow strip of yellow paper to make the concertina. Fold it to form a fan. When folding paper always use your thumbnail to press the fold firmly down.

5 Use glue to attach each end of the concertina to the end of the clown's arms.

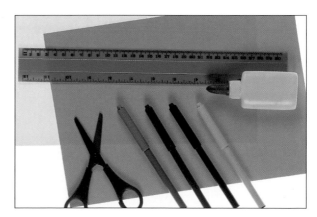

You will need:

Paper

Ruler

Felt-tip pens

Scissors

Glue

PAPER AND RIBBON
Gift Bags

Pack your Christmas gifts in these brightly colored gift bags. You can make them almost any size. Use one layer of paper for smaller bags and a double layer to make larger bags. You could decorate the paper before you begin. Make a stencil to decorate the paper if you are making a lot of bags all to match for party favors. The bag handles can be made from string or pretty ribbon. Have a look around for paper decorated on both sides, or use gold or silver paper.

You will need:
A selection of paper

Glue

Hole punch

Ribbon

1 Begin by folding the paper in by about one quarter of its length. Run your thumbnail along the fold to mark it well.

2 Turn the folded sheet of paper over and apply glue to one end.

3 Glue the edges together to form a cylinder shape. Allow the glue to dry.

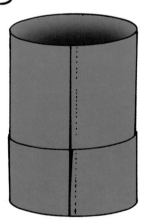

4 Flatten the cylinder shape. Run your thumbnail along the edges to make a good fold.

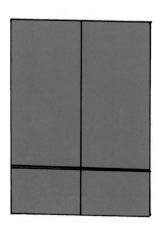

5 Fold about one quarter over on each side.

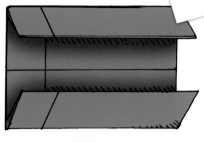

6 Open the two folds and press them inward. You should now have a bag shape.

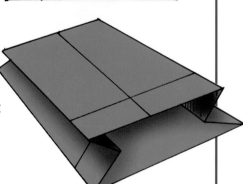

7 Make a fold upward to form the base of the bag. Glue it down.

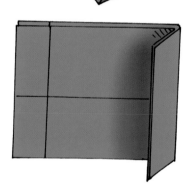

8 Use a hole punch to make holes to thread a ribbon through and make a handle.

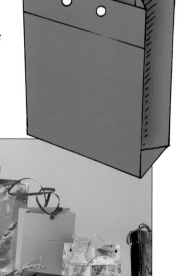

Cut-out Cards

Make a row of paper flowerpots and turn them into a birthday card, or a row of balloons to send as a party invitation. The Christmas tree cards can be decorated as brightly as you wish and the colourful fish swimming around in their bowls will brighten up the mantlepiece. Cut-out cards are quick and easy to make and decorate. When choosing the shape remember that the card will need to be cut out so draw a compact picture. A Christmas tree cut from plain white paper and decorated using a gold pen would be very stylish.

You will need:

Paper and thin cardboard

Felt-tip pens

Crayons

Scissors

Glue

Sequins to decorate

When decorating your cards try outlining colored-in pictures with a darker shade. This will accentuate the shapes and give the cards a professional finish.

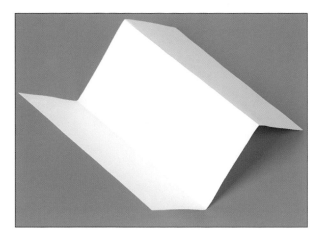

1 This card is easy to make and fun to color, you will need a rectangle of plain white paper. Fold the sheet of paper in three to make the card shape.

2 On the front of the card draw a pot of flowers. Make sure the flower pots are joined at the lip, or the card will fall apart when you cut it out.

3 Cut away the excess paper.

4 Color in your card using bright shades.

5 To make this cheery Christmas card use a sheet of green paper folded in three. Draw on the Christmas tree shape and cut it out. Take care to leave the branches joined together at the base of the tree. Glue on small flowerpots cut from paper for the trees to stand in and decorate the Christmas trees with sequins and shiny stars, glued on.

Notepaper

Fancy writing paper makes letterwriting more fun. You can decorate paper to suit the season: make bright sunny pictures for summer vacation letters and snowy scenes for winter times. You may like to experiment with other ideas. Maybe a seaside scene or some rolling hills covered in tiny black sheep and cows would suit a vacation mood. Choose bright coordinated colors and matching envelopes. Use the steely glints of shiny gold or silver pens to create a night scene or even to decorate a set of paper with a firework display.

You will need:

Paper

Felt-tip pens

Scissors

Glue

1 This summery style is made from green, blue, and white sheets of paper. Decorate the sky-blue sheet of paper first. Cut out small fluffy white clouds and glue them onto the sky.

3 This snowscene is decorated with a cheerful-looking snowman. Draw the snowman onto a white sheet of paper. Remember to draw the horizon onto the page.

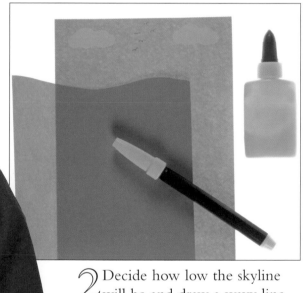

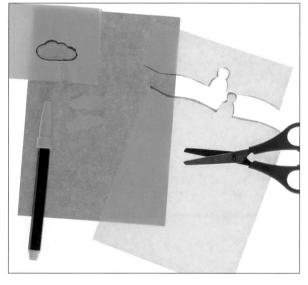

2 Decide how low the skyline will be and draw a wavy line across the green paper. Cut away the excess paper to leave grassy green hills. Lay one piece of paper on top of the other to create the scene.

4 Use scissors to cut out the snowman and lay the sheet of white paper onto the blue sky. Decorate the snowman using a black felt-tip pen, giving him a cheerful smile.

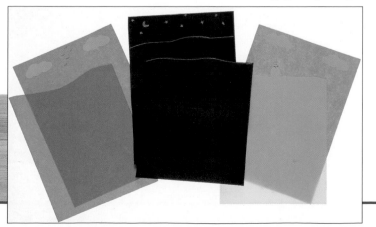

PAPER
Envelopes

You might have difficulty finding envelopes that are the correct size, especially if they are to match the paper and cards you have designed. Don't worry—there is no problem. Use these simple instructions and make envelopes to fit almost every size and shape of card. You could make the envelope from matching paper, patterned wrapping paper (you will need to attach a plain label for the address) or recycled paper. Decorate your home made envelopes using felt-tip pens, stickers, paint, or crayons. Remember to make the card first and use it to work around.

You will need:

A completed card

Paper

Scissors

Glue

Felt-tip pens

Any coloring materials should be waterproof as the envelope may get wet in the mail.

1 Place the card in the center of the paper. Fold the paper up, over the card.

2 Fold the envelope flap down, over the card.

3 Fold in the sides. Make sure the card fits the folded shape comfortably.

4 Cut away the excess paper from the front of the envelope.

5 Cut a flap shape.

6 Use glue to hold the envelope in shape.

CARDBOARD AND PAPER
Silhouettes

Making silhouettes was once a popular pastime. People would cut silhouettes in all sorts of shapes, profile outlines being very popular. Fine cutting skills are needed to make silhouettes. Practice on scraps of paper to learn the technique before you set to work on these shapes. Cut your silhouette from black paper and lay it on a light background. Try your hand at a larger silhouette, maybe a profile of yourself or a friend, to frame and hang on your bedroom wall. Silhouettes of candles and Christmas trees are very seasonal, while the pumpkin and cat cut-outs would make good Halloween party invitations.

You will need:
Paper
Wax or pencil crayon
Scissors
Glue

1 Fold a sheet of black paper in half. Draw half a butterfly on to one side of the folded shape. Cut it out. It is possible to cut out the butterfly shape freehand.

Make a card from a folded sheet of paper and glue a piece of red paper onto the cover of the card. Glue the butterfly silhouette onto the piece of red paper.

2 This Halloween card is made with a bright yellow silhouette. Use a card made from yellow paper and glue on a black background, leaving a yellow border around the edge of the card. Fold a small piece of yellow paper in half and draw on half of the pumpkin face. Cut it out and glue it onto the black background.

Stained Glass

Create your own stained glass pictures with colored plastic wrapping. Placed where the light shines through them these cards are most effective. Colored wrapping film is available from craft shops; however, you might want to save candy wrappers and keep an eye out for colored clear plastic to recycle. The holly leaves make a good Christmas card. You can have fun decorating the card with colored glitter glue.

You will need:

Black paper

Felt-tip pen

Scissors

Colored clear wrapping

Glue and glitter glue

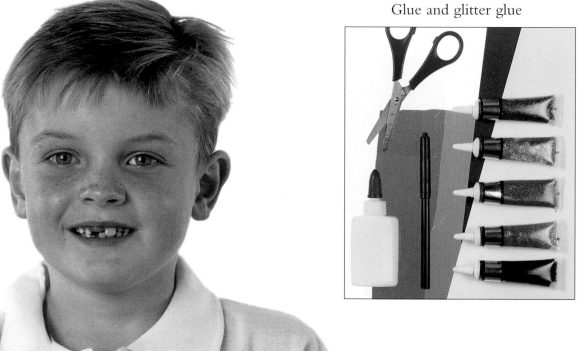

1 To make this clear blue fish bowl card begin by folding a sheet of white paper in half. Draw on a simple fish bowl shape and cut it out.

2 Cut a rectangle of blue colored wrapping slightly larger than the fish bowl. Glue the rectangle onto the inside of the card, covering the fish bowl shape.
Fold the card closed. You will decorate the cover of the card.

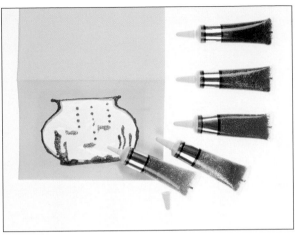

3 Use glitter glue to fill the bowl with fish, colored seaweed, and pebbles. Don't forget to paint on air bubbles. Decorate the edge of the bowl as well.

4 You will need a sheet of black paper folded in half to make the holly card. Begin by cutting out the holly leaves and berries. Cut green colored wrapping slightly larger than the cut-out leaves and glue it to the inside of the card. Use red wrapping for the berries. Fold the card to close it and decorate the stained glass-effect card with colored glitter glue.

If you do not have glitter glue, make your own. Use ordinary glue and mix in an equal amount of fine glitter. Use a fine paintbrush to apply the glitter glue to your model or card.

TISSUE PAPER
Stenciled Wrapping Paper

Stenciling is a quick and effective way to decorate wrapping paper and gift tags. Use gold or silver paint to turn plain tissue paper into expensive looking wrapping paper. The stencils are easily cut from small sheets of paper folded in half. You could make matching gift wrap and tags to suit any event or gift. Once you have mastered the art of stenciling you may want to try using two colors. It is also useful to remember that other coloring materials and methods are good for stenciling. You don't have to use paint—try wax crayons, for example.

You will need:

Paper

Pencil

Scissors

Tissue paper

Paint

Saucer

Sponge

Hole punch

Thread

Always protect your work surface with newspaper or a vinyl cloth.

Remember to wipe up any spills as they happen. A good craftsperson leaves a tidy work surface.

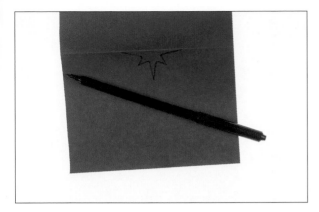

1 To make a stencil you will need a small sheet of paper. Fold it in half and draw on half of the picture, in this case half of the star, as shown in the picture above.

2 Use the scissors to cut the star out, taking care not to leave any jagged edges and not to cut into the paper. If you do, the stencil paint may come through.

3 Spread a sheet of tissue paper across your work surface. Pour a little paint onto the saucer, spread it on the sponge, damping the sponge down. Place the stencil on some rough paper and practice until you are confident.

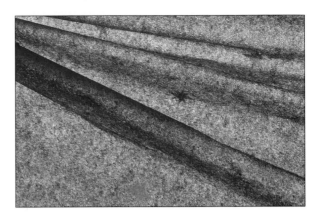

4 Stencil on the stars taking care not to smudge the paint when you lift the stencil off the paper. Hang your stenciled paper up to dry. It is a good idea to make quite a few sheets at a time, as well as matching gift tags.

5 Use paper to make these matching gift tags. Cut them out with scissors. Stencil on the star and leave to dry.

6 Use a hole punch to make a hole for the thread to tie the tag onto the gift.

Tissue Paper Cards

Tissue paper comes in such a wide range of colors, it is easy to tear and sticks with the minimum of glue. When decorating cards there is no end to the number of ways you can use tissue paper. These cards are made from torn strips of tissue and layered to create blended colors and a simple design. The colors are bright and breezy and very stylish. Have a go at layering colors yourself. Create a natural looking landscape with torn or cut greens, blues and browns.

You will need:

Colored paper

Tissue paper

Scissors

Glue

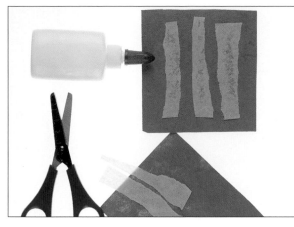

1 Fold a piece of colored paper in half to form the card. Tear off pieces of lime green tissue paper and use small amounts of glue to stick them onto the card.

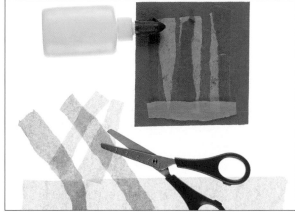

2 Now layer on strips of pink tissue paper and follow these with a border of blue tissue paper strips. When the glue has set, your card is ready for you to sign and send to a friend.

3 This eyecatching Valentine card is easy to make. You will need to layer 4 pieces of red tissue paper together, fold them in half, and carefully tear out a heart shape. The border of the card is made from scissor-cut pieces of red tissue paper.

PAPIER-MÂCHÉ
Bon Bon Plate

Make this golden plate and load it with candies for the party table. The plate is made using a china or metal plate with a wide edge as a mold. Use the plate to hold wrapped sweets or small cakes in paper cases. A gold plate of home made goodies would make a lovely gift.

1 The plate will be your mold for the papier-mâché. Begin by covering the plate completely with plastic wrap. Use white glue to stick a layer of paper squares onto the plastic wrap covered plate. You will need to stick the squares completely up to the edge. Leave it to dry and then apply the next layer of newspaper squares. You will need to stick on at least 6 layers to make a plate strong enough to carry the candies.

2 When the papier-mâché is completely dry lift off the plate and peel away the clingfilm. Cut a zigzag pattern around the edge of the plate and paint the plate gold.

You will need:
A plate with a wide edge
Newspaper squares
Glue
Plastic wrap
Paintbrush
Scissors
Gold paint

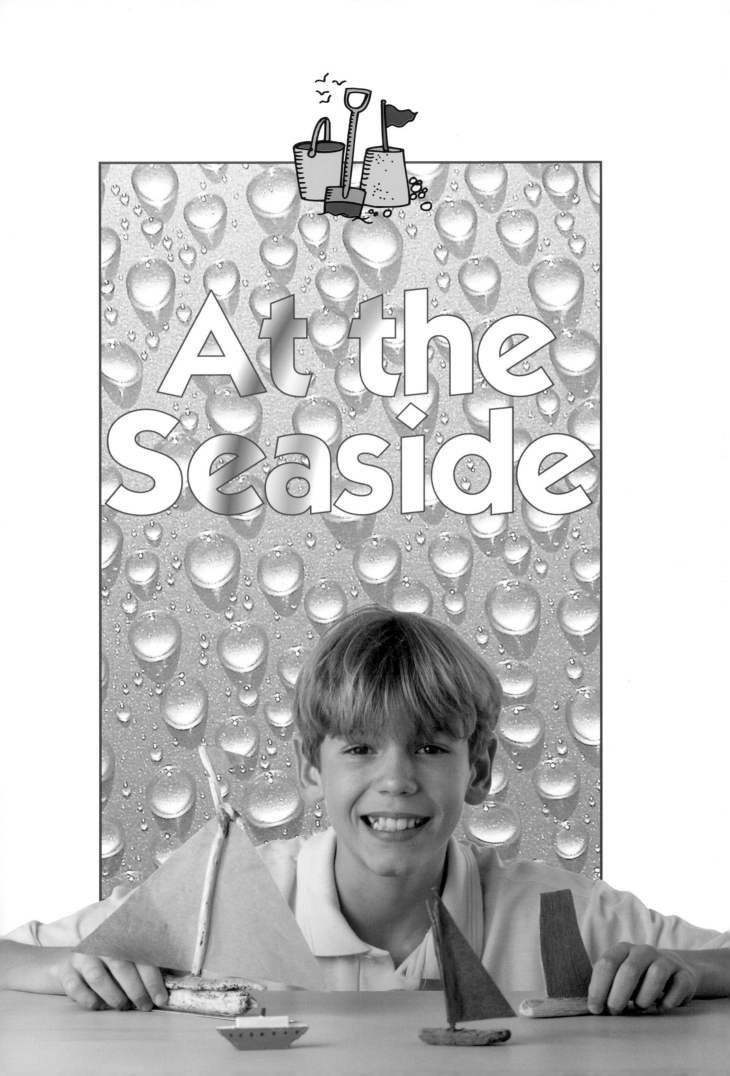

At the Seaside

Boats

When you go for a walk along the beach keep your eyes open for unusual items. This is called beachcombing. Driftwood is often washed up on the shore and collecting it is great fun, but what can you do with all those oddly shaped pieces of wood? Making small boats is one way of using them. The sails and flags can be cut from colored tissue paper. You could make a miniature fleet of small craft and feature them on a sunny windowsill. You will need your imagination to create interesting boats, masts, and sails. If you want to join pieces together, you will need to use a strong glue. Driftwood often looks good left a natural color. However, it sometimes needs decorating.

You will need:

Selection of driftwood pieces

Tissue paper

Sturdy scissors

Glue

Tissue paper

Paint

Paintbrush

Emery board

1 When making driftwood boats spend a lot of time planning the best use of particular pieces of wood you may have found. Occasionally you will find one that needs just a sail or a dot of paint to turn it into an interesting craft.

Sometimes you will need to change the shape of a piece of wood; strong scissors may do. Try using an emery board or a small piece of sandpaper to shape pieces to fit neatly together. Most of all you need to enjoy being creative with your seaside materials.

When beachcombing take care you do not injure yourself. Wear beach shoes and use rubber gloves. Check found items for nails and do not touch anything you don't recognize.

SHELLS AND DRIFTWOOD
Mobiles

Beachcombing can be very rewarding—the tides wash all sorts of things up on the beach. Interesting pieces of driftwood and pretty shells can be turned into mobiles and hung up as a reminder of seaside days. When making a mobile you need a shapely piece of driftwood to start with. You can use thread or string to tie on attractive shells and stones. The mobile needs to be well balanced. Check this by hanging the mobile up as soon as you have a few pieces tied on, adjusting the weight as you go. Paint on a layer of varnish for a glossy look.

You will need:

Driftwood	Shells
Pebbles	Thread
Small nails	Paintbrush
Scissors	Varnish

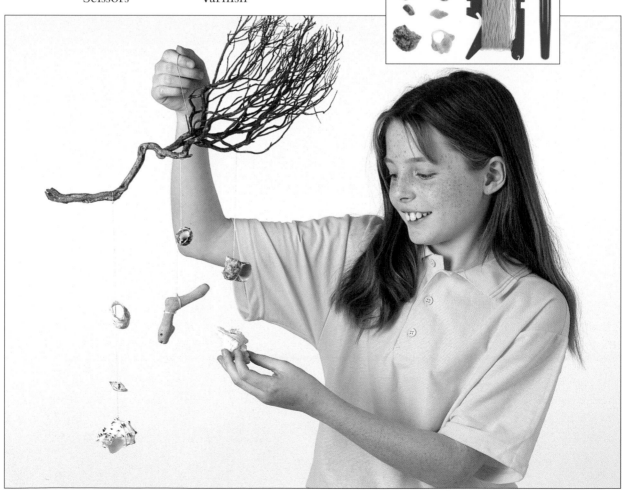

1 You will need a piece of driftwood and some small nails to make the hanger for this mobile. Use a hammer to knock the nails into position.

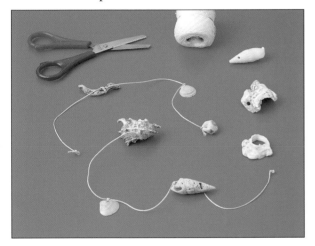

2 Tie good knots when attaching the shells and driftwood to the string. Consider how the mobile will appear when hung up when you do this.

4 This mobile is made by tying the weighted strings directly onto the driftwood. You could use loops and hang the strings on or tie them on with small tight knots. You will need to check the mobile for balance as you make it. When the mobile is complete you might want to paint on a layer of varnish to give the shells a glossy finish.

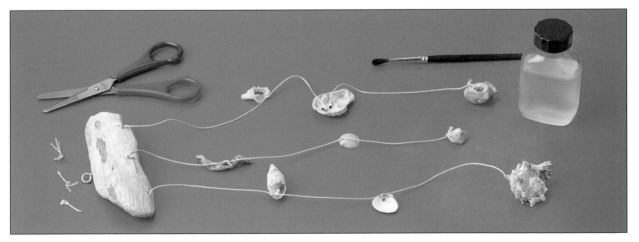

3 Once you are happy with the balance of the mobile, paint a layer of varnish onto the shells. Hang up your mobile and let it remind you of a very happy holiday.

FABRIC PAINT
Beach Shoes

Beach shoes are very useful, but usually come in rather dull black or white. Use fabric paints to decorate them. The fabric paints used in this project are available from craft and fabric shops and are easy to use. It is a good idea to practice first on a piece of cardboard. Try out a few designs. Fish or flowers make good patterns. Choose a pattern that is easy to repeat.

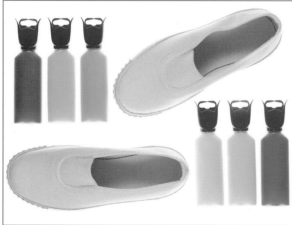

You will need:
Canvas shoes

Fabric paint

Be sure to clean up any spills as they occur. Don't forget to leave your work area tidy.

1 These shoes have been painted with a seaside theme. Take care not to smudge the decoration as you go along. When you have completed the first shoe use it as a pattern for the other one. In that way you will be able to create a matching design. Once your shoes are decorated leave them in a safe place to dry completely before you wear them on your next beachcombing expedition.

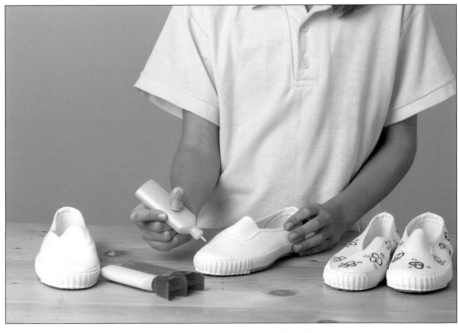

2 Flower patterns are easy to draw on and look very attractive. Decorate a pair of shoes to wear during the summer months. You could take inspiration from a special dress or T-shirt.

Lighthouse

Models are great fun to make. This lighthouse standing on a rocky island surrounded by the blue sea looks very realistic. Spend some time planning your model, then make a rough drawing. If you have been to the seaside you may recall a particular lighthouse or other seaside scene which you could re-create in miniature. When you are away on vacation you may want to collect a few pebbles and some sand to use to make the model when you return home. It is amazing what you can achieve with some plaster, pebbles, and paint.

You will need:

A cardboard lid

Margarine tub

Stones

Pebbles

Plaster-of-Paris

Bowl and spatula

Air-hardening clay

Glue

Paint and paintbrushes

1 Place the margarine tub toward one end of the box lid. Position the stones; they will jut out of the "water" so need to be quite tall. When you are happy with the arrangement mix up the plaster-of-Paris in the bowl and pour it over everything.

2 You will now need to make the lighthouse. Use some air-hardening clay and make a long cylinder shape, wider at one end than the other. The room at the top will need to be made separately. Leave the pieces to dry in a warm airy spot.

3 When the plaster and the lighthouse pieces are dry you can glue everything in place. Use strong glue. Leave the model in a warm airy spot to dry.

4 Spread a thick layer of glue where ever you need to place the small pebbles. These will give the impression of rocks. A few on top of the island will look good.

5 Once your model is dry it is ready to paint and decorate. Have fun and use plenty of imagination to create a realistic-looking rocky, seaside scene.

Photo Album

Beach vacations are best remembered in photographs. Make one of these albums to keep your photographs safe. Choose bright nautical colors; blue and yellow are fun. The albums are made from cardboard and colored cord holds the pages together. Try making a seaside collage to decorate the cover. A beach scene or a gaily colored yacht would look good.

You will need:

Thin colored cardboard

Colored paper

Scissors

Hole punch

Cord

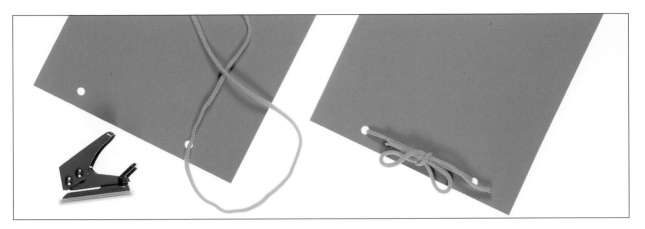

1 Cut the covers and pages to size. Use the hole punch to make holes through the covers and pages. You will need to take care that they line up. Thread colored cord through the holes to hold the album together securely and tie a bow.

2 To make the photograph holders cut a narrow strip of paper. Fold the paper inwards to create a corner sleeve. Cut away any excess paper and glue the sleeve onto the page. Do this four times, one for each corner then insert the photograph.

3 Decorate the cover of your album with an attractive seaside collage. Use colored paper to create this yacht and cut out a row of waves to glue along the bottom of the page.

Seaside Jewelry

Shells, attractive stones, and small pieces of driftwood can be made up into earrings and pendants. Use fine wire and thread to assemble the jewelry. You can also buy ready-made clasps and earring backs from craft shops. These are called jewelry findings. Look along the seashore for two matching shells with small holes in and make them up into earrings. As you walk along the beach keep an eye out for interestingly shaped, colored stones.

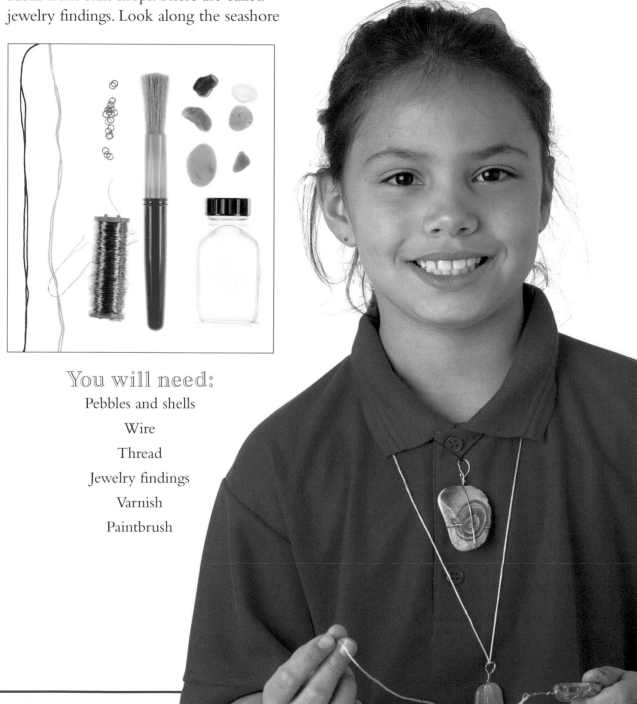

You will need:

Pebbles and shells

Wire

Thread

Jewelry findings

Varnish

Paintbrush

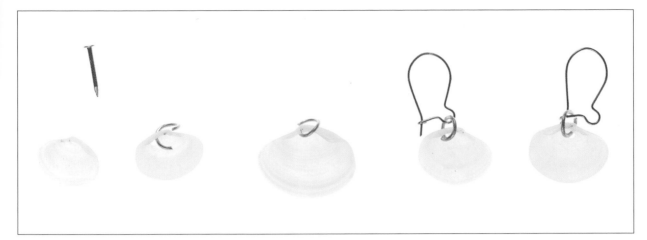

1 These dainty shell earrings are easy to make. These shells have tiny holes naturally occurring in them. However you may have to use a press-together jewelry binding to hold the shell in place. Attach the earring hook to each shell and you have a pretty pair of earrings to wear as a reminder of your visit to the beach.

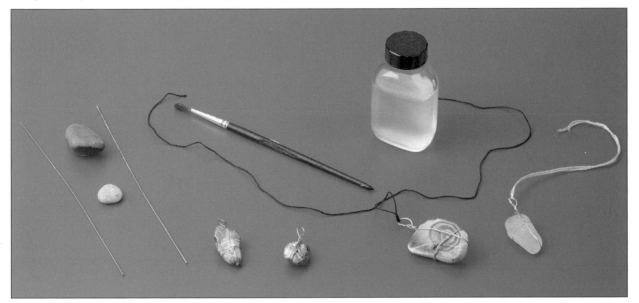

2 To make these pendants you will need some attractively marked pebbles. Use clear varnish painted over the pebbles to bring out the rich patterns (clear nail varnish works just as well).

Wind a piece of wire around the pebble and finish with a loop at the top. Attach a piece of thread to the loop and use this to hang your pendant around your neck.

Check that it is okay to pick up shells along the beach where you are.

Three-in-a-row

Three-in-a-row is a good game to both make and to play. Once you have made a board you can make a selection of counters, different sets to suit different occasions. The boards are made from cardboard and craft wood while the counters are made from oven-bake clay.

Matching shells make good counters too. To play the game you need two players. Each player takes turns placing a counter on the board. You must both try to take defensive action when it's your turn, to prevent the other player from getting three-in-a-row. The first player to get a row wins.

You will need:

Thick colored cardboard

Craft strip wood

Scissors

Paintbrush

Oven-bake clay

Shells

Glue

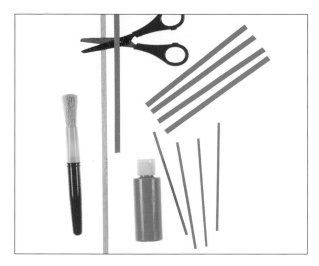

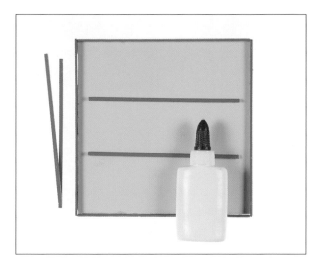

1 Begin by painting the craft strip wood in your chosen color. Choose a color that coordinates with the thick colored card you will use for the base of the board. Leave it until it is thoroughly dry.

3 Attach the sides to the board with glue. Cut the board markings from thin strip wood and glue these in place. Make sure you position them correctly on the board.

2 The size of your games board is decided by the piece of thick colored cardboard. This will need to be square. Cut the sides for your board to length from the craft strip wood, using your board as a pattern.

4 Glue on the cross markings. Don't worry if your paintwork gets a little scratched. Once the glue is dry you can use paint to touch up any spots that might need it.

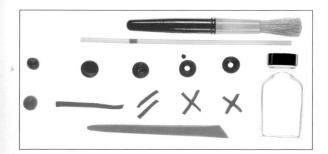

5 These tic-tac-toe counters are made from oven-bake clay. Use different colors and check that the counters fit the available space on the board. Try your hand at making little boats, dolphins, and starfish as a variation from flat counters.

Paperweights

Pebble painting is fun and a good rainy day activity. Collect pebbles along the beach and save them. When you want to enjoy a quiet time get out the paints and your imagination, and make these attractive paperweights. You could paint a tiny row of pebble cottages (use a fine paintbrush to paint on tiny windows and doors) and little rose bushes along the cottage front. Or try your hand at painting a tiny kitten on a pebble or a fish or even a skeleton.

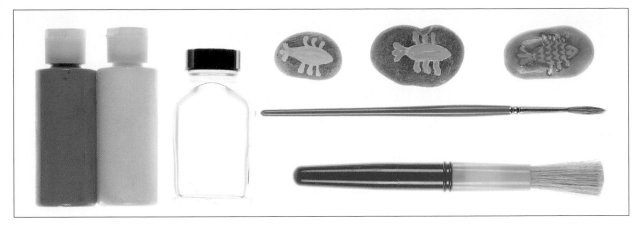

1 These interesting decorations need a little time and practice. Wash and dry the pebbles before you begin. Use a fine paintbrush to paint in the detail. Once you are happy with your chosen decoration and the paint has dried, add a layer of varnish.

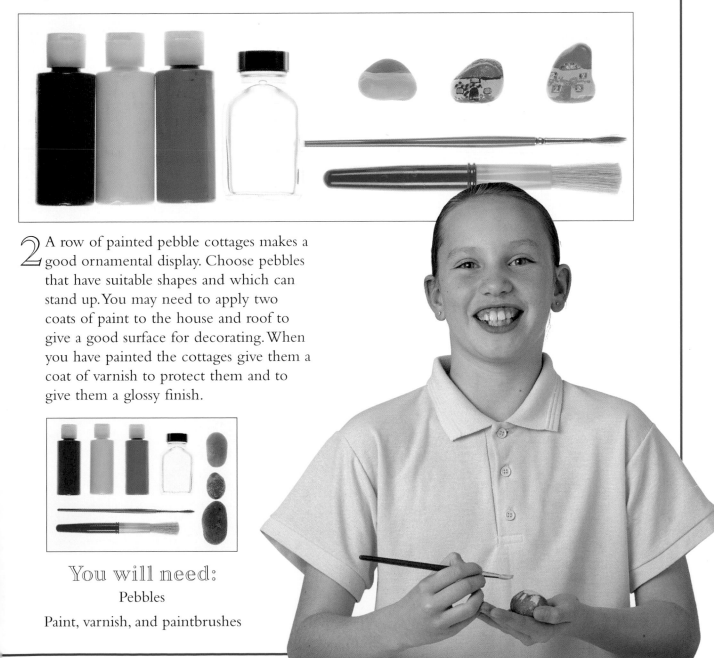

2 A row of painted pebble cottages makes a good ornamental display. Choose pebbles that have suitable shapes and which can stand up. You may need to apply two coats of paint to the house and roof to give a good surface for decorating. When you have painted the cottages give them a coat of varnish to protect them and to give them a glossy finish.

You will need:
Pebbles

Paint, varnish, and paintbrushes

MOSAIC
Tablemats

Mosaics are usually created using small square tiles. To make these tablemats we have cut lots of small squares from paper and used them glued onto sugar paper to create a fishy picture. Choose bright colors to create your pictures. Squares cut from magazine pictures can also be used to make mosaics.

The important thing to remember, when making a mosaic, is to keep the lines straight. This gives the impression of tiles all lined up. Use a ruler and pencil to make markings on your paper so that you can keep the squares neat and in order.

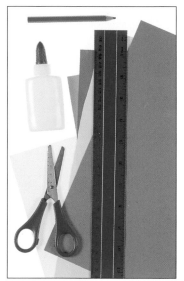

You will need:
Paper
Ruler
Pencil
Scissors
Glue

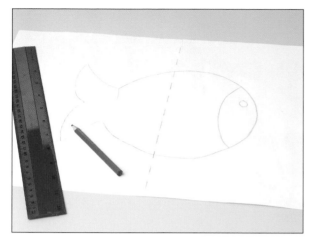

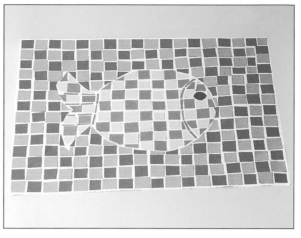

1 Begin by drawing a simple outline of a fish on your paper. Make sure that the picture is centrally placed.

4 Your finished fish mosaic should look something like this. You could make a set of table mats for the family.

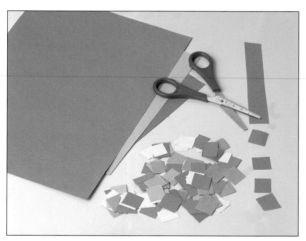

2 Use the ruler and pencil to measure out squares and cut them out in your chosen colours. You will need a lot of squares.

5 For a special event you might want to decorate some table napkins to match your table mats. Use paper and create pretty collage pictures.

3 Glue on the squares. Begin in a corner of the picture and try to work from one side of the picture to the other.

Flowerpots

Flowerpots look good sitting along a sunny windowsill. Fill them with brightly colored flowers to bring a little of the garden indoors. These pots are decorated with shells bought from a specialist craft shop. The shells are all recycled. The creatures that used to live in them are used as food in some countries and the shells simply thrown away. Ask at your local craft shops for them. If you gather them yourself, always check that you are allowed to on that particular beach.

You will need:

Shells

Terra-cotta pot or container to recycle

Grout

Spatula

Paint

Paintbrush

Glue

Varnish

1 Choose your plant pot and shells. Use a spatula to apply a layer of grout along the rim of the pot. Press the shells firmly into the grout. Leave the grout to dry. When it is dry you may want to apply a little varnish to bring out the colors of the shells.

2 These pretty pink pots have been decorated with tiny shells. Begin by painting the pot pink. You may need two coats of paint. After the paint is dry use strong glue to attach the shells. When the glue has set apply a layer of varnish to the shells.

CARDBOARD AND GLITTER
Aquarium

The fish floating in this model aquarium are made from thin cardboard and decorated with paint and glitter. They shimmer through the weed and clear blue sea very realistically when you gently shake the box. Use a large shoe box to make the aquarium. You could make a shoal of tiny fish to weave their way through the weed. The fish are suspended from the ceiling of the box with thin gold thread which is almost invisible. Place a few rocks and shells in the bottom of the box. If you have one, a model shipwreck would make an attractive feature.

You will need:

Large shoebox

Scissors

Paint & paintbrush

Blue plastic film

Tissue paper

Thin cardboard and paper

Felt-tip pens

Glue

Glitter

Gold thread

Pebbles

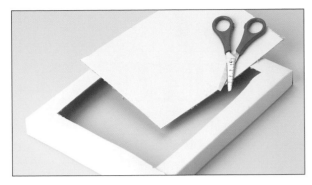

1 Cut a rectangle from the box lid.

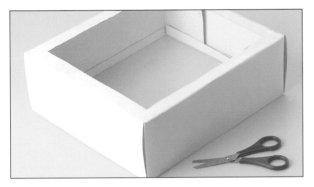

2 Cut a rectangle from the base of the box.

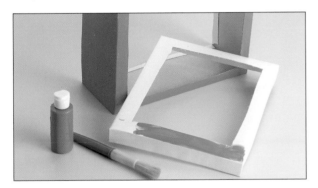

3 Paint the box and lid blue, inside and out.

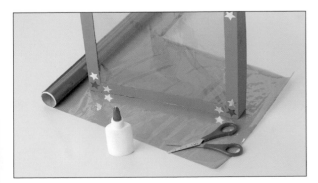

4 Glue blue film over the cut-out spaces.

5 Cut strips of tissue paper for weeds. Glue them in place suspended from the roof of the aquarium. Use two colors of green.

6 Draw fish on the thin cardboard and decorate them with paint and glitter. Attach them to the lid of the box with gold thread.

STICKS, STRING, AND CARDBOARD
Fishing Game

Fishing games always go down well at parties and games evenings. This fishing game is quite easy to make. The fish hooks and the fish mouths are made from paper clips. You could also make fish in two colors or make several different sea creatures, such as fish and starfish. Then players can see how many of each they can "catch" in a given time. Another game might be to give each fish a value, adding the values at the end of the game to see which "catch" is worth the most. This would introduce gamesmanship as each player goes for the highest value catch.

You will need:

Plate

Thick cardboard

Thin cardboard

Scissors

Glue

Tape

Ruler

Felt tips

Sticks

String

Paper clips

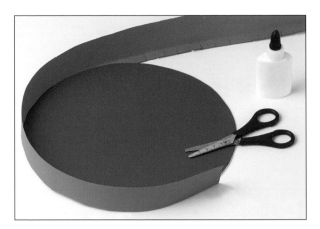

1 Use a plate as an outline for a circular shape on a piece of thick cardboard. Cut out the circle to be the base of the pond. Measure out a long strip of thin card for the sides. Tape it to the base.

2 The sides of the pond will prevent the fish from jumping out! Use colored tape or felt-tip pens to decorate the sides.

3 Draw the fish and starfish on a piece of thick cardboard and decorate them using felt-tip pens. Cut them out. You will need to make quite a few fish and starfish.

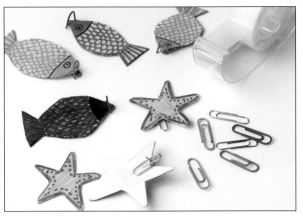

4 Now make the loops on the decorated stars and fish from paper clips. You will need to fold up a section of the paper clip and attach it with tape to the fish and starfish.

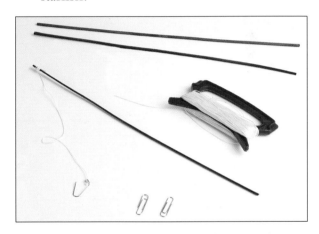

5 The fishing rods are made from garden sticks. Tie a piece of string to one end of each stick and a paper clip to the end of each piece of string. Shape the paper clip into a hook.

PAPER AND COLORED PENCILS

Lettercards

Making lettercards is easy, fun and turns letterwriting into a creative activity. Make these lettercards before you set off on your seaside holiday. Then you will have a supply to send to friends when you are on vacation. Decorate your lettercards with flowers, fish, tiny boats, or other seaside scenes. You will need a large dinner plate to draw around. Once your lettercard is decorated and written you can fold it up ready to post as it turns into its own envelope. Lettercards are good for writing thank you letters or short wish-you-were-here notes while you are on holiday. A set of decorated lettercards would make a good gift.

You will need:

Paper

Plate

Coloring pencils

Small rectangular box

Stickers

1 Place the plate on the sheet of white paper and use it to draw a circle.

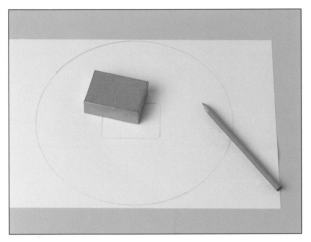

2 Place the small rectangular box in the centre of the circle and draw around it. This will be the address label.

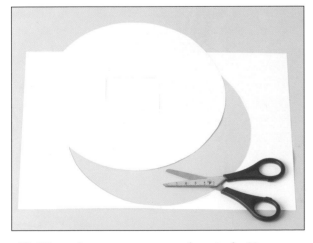

3 Use scissors to cut out the circle. Your lettercard is now ready to decorate. You need to decorate around the address label.

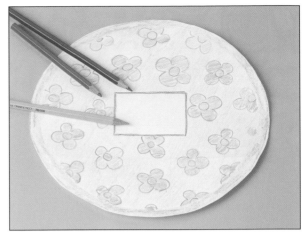

4 The pattern on this lettercard is decorated in seaside colors of blue and yellow.

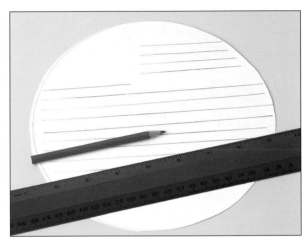

5 Turn the lettercard over to the blank side This is where you will write your letter. Rule lines to write on.

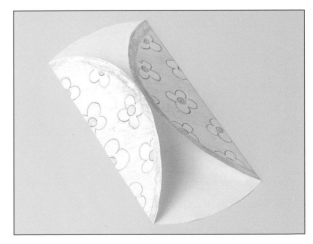

6 When you have written your letter, fold the sides inward and use a sticker to hold the lettercard closed.

Treasure Boxes

S hells can be used decoratively in so many ways. In this project they are used to decorate a small storage box and to make a pretty circular picture frame. You will need an empty cheese box and some shells to make the storage box plus some grout or strong glue to attach the shells. You can arrange them in a regular pattern or randomly over the lid. The picture frame is made from thin cardboard.

You will need:

Empty cheese box

Selection of shells

Grout

Spatula

Thin cardboard

Scissors

Varnish

Paintbrush

If you do not have any grout you could use some strong glue.

1 First check that the box is clean. Before you begin, experiment with the design. Lay the shells on the lid without any grout. When you are happy with the design spread a layer of grout across the box lid using the spatula and gently press the shells in place.

3 To make this pretty shell encrusted picture frame you will need a circle of thin cardboard with a hole cut out of the centre. This will make the frame shape. Apply a layer of grout using the spatula and gently press the shells into an attractive pattern around the edge.

2 Leave the box in a warm airy spot to dry. You will need to give the shell covered box plenty of time to dry off. When it is dry paint on a layer of varnish to give the shells an attractive finish.

4 When the grout has dried the frame is ready for a layer of varnish. This will protect it and bring out the colors. Now you can insert a photograph and hang up the frame or use it as a small paperweight.

Pencil Wallet

Clear plastic wallets can be decorated with glass paints to create your own personal style. This wallet has been designed to give the impression of a fish bowl, with two brightly colored fish. File wallets can be personalized with glass paint. Black outliner is great for a labeling design. Different subject folders would look good with a decorated title. Enjoy practicing your creative skills on different plastic containers.

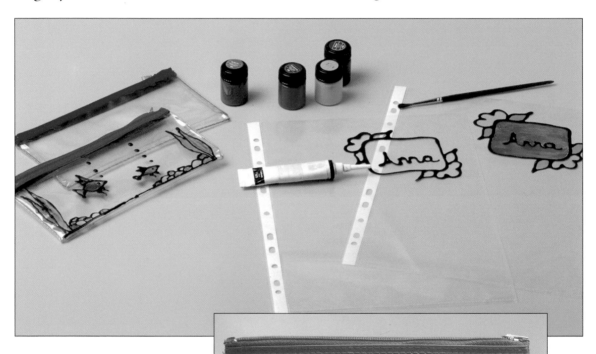

1 Before you start on a design make sure the plastic wallet or folder is completely clean. Try out a few design ideas on paper first, practicing the shapes. Use the outliner to mark out your design on the wallet or folder. The outliner will take an hour or so to dry. When it is dry paint on the color with a clean dry brush. Do one color at a time and clean the brush carefully between colors.

You will need:
A clear plastic wallet
Glass paints
Black outliner
Kitchen paper to mop up any spills

Toys and Games

BOTTLE TOPS
Snake

This beautiful sinuous snake can be made from bottle tops. You will need to collect a lot of bottle tops, so it may be worth asking friends to save them for you. By combining different colored tops you could create a multi-colored snake and if you saved only one color of bottle tops your snake would still be dramatic. The silver shimmers and the closely fitted bottle tops give the appearance of scales when wriggled along the floor. The snake's head is made from a cork and his bright red tongue is a piece of felt, cut to shape and pushed into the cork.

You will need:
Hammer

Large nail

Piece of wood

Bottle tops

Strong string

Scissors

Cork

Glue

Paint & paintbrushes

Small piece of felt

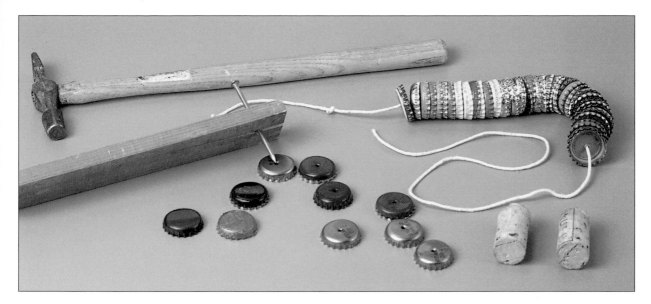

1 Hammer a nail through a piece of wood near its end. You can then hold the wood and position the nail to make the hole in the center of the bottle top.

When all the bottle tops have holes in them thread them onto the string. Think about your color coordination. A snake like this one will need approximately 70 bottle tops.

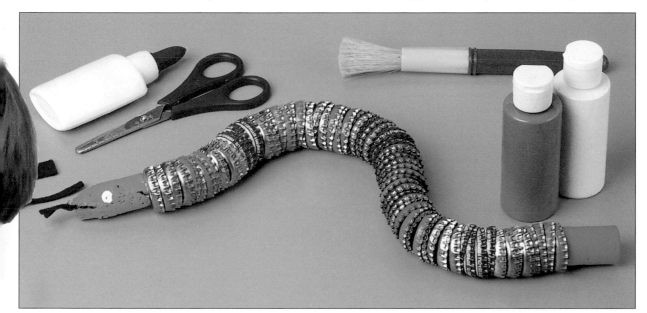

2 Attach a piece of cork to each end of the string of bottle tops. One end will be the tail—paint it green. The other end will be the head—paint this green also and add two spots for the eyes. Cut a small piece of felt into the shape of a snake's tongue and press it into the cork with the point of the nail.

OVEN-BAKE CLAY
Pocket Pets

These cute little pets don't need feeding or cleaning out, just a little loving! The animals are made from oven-bake clay, simply shaped and pressed together. Give the dog big soppy eyes by using a white flattened ball and laying a black eyespot on top of it. Place the black eyespot carefully as that is what gives them character.

The dog collar is another important item. Be sure to give your pets a tag with your telephone number on it in case they wander off! Make a water bowl and bone—and maybe a few doggy toys would be a good idea. The kennels are made from recycled milk or juice cartons. Paint them in bright colors and write your pet's name above the entrance.

You will need:
Oven-bake clay

Modeling tool

Empty milk or juice carton

Scissors

Paint

Paintbrush

Large flat lid for
the cat's basket

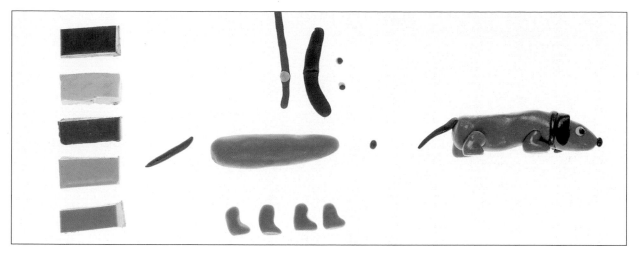

1 To make the dog, soften the clay between your fingers then shape the body and feet. Take a small piece of dark brown clay and roll out a thin tail. Make a flattened sausage shape for the ears and lastly make the eyes and collar. Assemble your little pet and bake it in the oven according to the manufacturer's instructions.

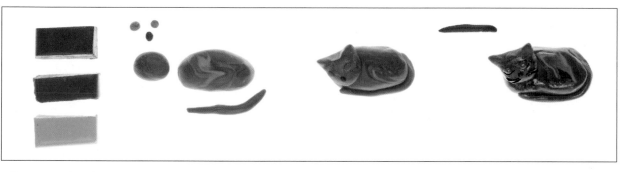

2 To make the cat you will need orange, yellow, and brown clay. Roughly mix equal quantities of orange and yellow clay. Shape the body first and then the head. Use your fingertips to pinch out the ears. Roll out thin pieces of brown clay to make the cat's whiskers and eyes and position them on the face. When you are happy with the shape of your pet, bake it in the oven according to the manufacturer's instructions.

3 To make this roomy kennel you will need an empty milk or juice carton. Cut out the shape and mark the entrance. Paint the kennel in attractive colors. You might want to write your pet's name above the entrance hole.

If you don't have any oven-bake clay make your pets from Plasticine.

PLASTIC CONTAINERS AND OVEN-BAKE CLAY
Bowling

Enjoy a game of bowling whenever you like with these brightly decorated recycled drink containers. You will need six containers to make a set. Paint them in bright colors and decorate them with colored stars. If they get knocked over too easily, pour some sand into each one to make them heavier. Mini- or table-bowling can also be fun. You could make a set to take away on vacation. They are made from oven bake clay. Take turns with a friend to see how many skittles you can knock down with each shot.

You will need:
Empty drink containers

Paint

Paintbrushes

Sand, for weight

To make mini-bowling you will need:

Oven-bake clay

1 Wash out the drink containers well. Leave upside down to drain. Screw the lids on tightly and your skittles are ready for painting. Begin by painting a base coat.

You may need two layers of paint. When the base coat is dry, paint on the decoration. When all your skittles are painted and decorated they are ready for use.

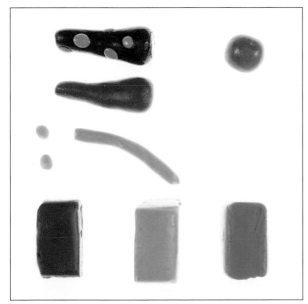

2 To make these mini-bowling pins you will need oven-bake clay in three colors. Divide the clay into equal pieces and shape the skittles. Use oven bake clay of a different color to make flattened ball shapes and press them onto the bowling pins. Shape a ball and when your ball and bowling pins are ready, bake in the oven according to the manufacturer's directions. You might want to decorate a small box in which to store your mini-bowling pins.

A set of mini-bowling pins would make a good Christmas cracker gift or party favor.

A full size set of bowling pins could be used at a school sports day or fund-raising event.

Magic Pictures

This fishy picture changes from black and white to color quite magically. Make one to delight a younger brother or sister. Choose your picture carefully: an empty black and white hillside could turn into a green pasture covered with sheep, or a bare table top could have a birthday cake appear on it.

Use brightly colored felt-tip pens to color your picture. It is a good idea to keep the shapes simple. If you don't have a plastic folder you might be able to recycle a piece of clear plastic from a carton.

You will need:

Thin cardboard or paper

Scissors

Marker and felt-tip pens

Plastic folder

Tape

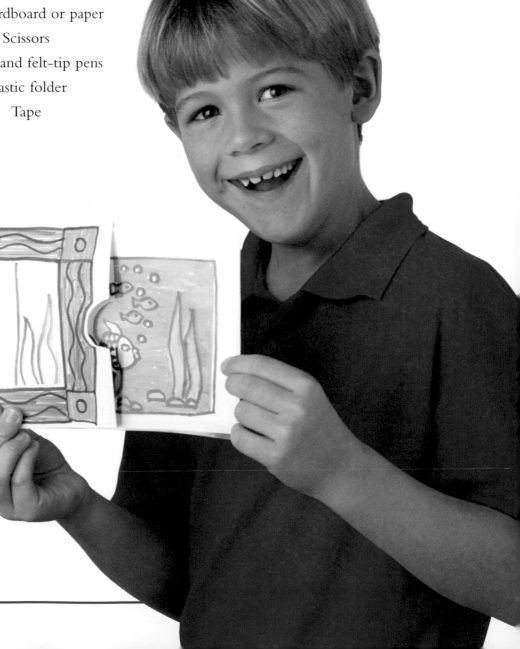

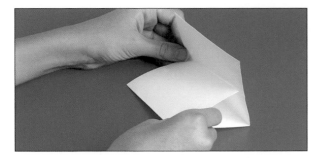

1 Take a sheet of thin cardboard or paper and fold it carefully into three equal sections as shown in the picture.

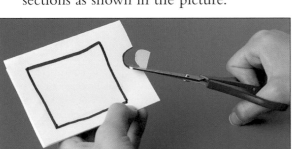

2 On the front flap mark out a rectangle and the finger grip space. Cut away the finger grip space.

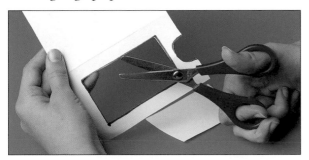

3 Open out the cardboard and cut out the rectangle. This is the front of the card.

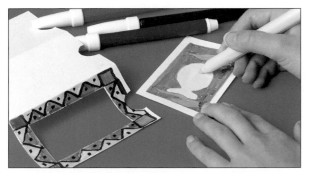

4 Draw a decorative border on this front frame. Cut a separate piece of paper the same size as one section of the card and draw on your design, using felt-tip pens.

5 Slip your picture into the plastic folder with the top against a fold. Trim the plastic to the picture. Stick the back to the plastic.

6 Use a marker pen to draw an outline of the picture on the plastic. Now take your card and open it out flat.

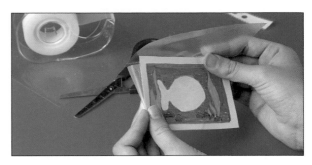

7 Fold the bottom flap into the middle. Slip the plastic-covered picture over the bottom flap. The bottom flap is now between the colored picture and the outlined picture on the plastic flap. Fold the top flap down over the plastic. Grip the plastic and paper and pull; the picture will appear in color as you pull it out.

CARD AND OVEN-BAKE CLAY
Games Board

This neat little games board is made from thick cardboard and a piece of narrow craft wood. You will need a little time and patience to paint the squares neatly but it is worthwhile when you consider the entertainment you will get from a home made games board. Here we show how you can make home-made checkers from oven-bake clay. You could use two colors of buttons or pebbles instead. Maybe you have a small set of chess pieces at home that could be used. A personalized board would make a lovely present.

You will need:

A small board-shaped piece of thick cardboard

Paint & paintbrushes

Pencil

Ruler

Scissors

Thin piece of strip wood from a craft shop

Glue

Oven-bake clay

Match box

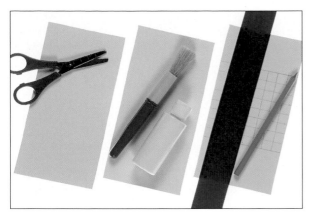

1 Paint the card in a light color. Paint the strip wood in a darker color. Leave to dry in a safe spot. When the paint is dry, carefully mark out the games board with eight rows of eight squares. Use the ruler to measure the squares. Leave space at each end of the board to keep pieces not in use during the game.

2 When you are satisfied with the marked areas, paint in the darker color. When the paint is dry, use the scissors to cut the strip wood and glue into shape to form an edge around the board. Decorate the board with an attractive pattern at each end and touch up any parts of the edging that need painting.

3 Shape the checkers from oven-bake clay. You will need eight counters in each color. It is best to roll out a sausage shape of clay and cut slices to size. Bake them in the oven following the manufacturer's directions. Paint a small matchbox in the darker color and decorate it to match your games board. Use the box to store your checkers.

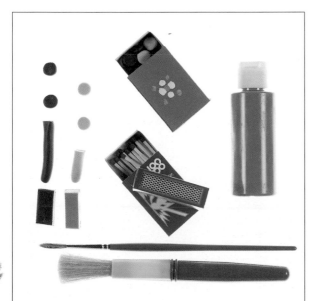

If you had an old tray you might want to recycle it into a games board. Ask an adult for help; you may need to sand the tray down with sandpaper first as well as decorate it using several coats of paint!

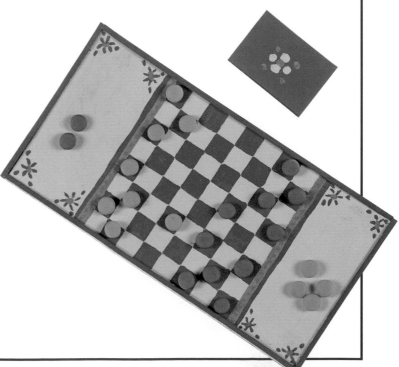

Dollhouse

Make a cute little dollhouse for a miniature doll or bear to live in. This house is made from two boxes. Use any card you may have over to make miniature furniture. You may want to have a look round for some small matchboxes or other containers to recycle as furniture. Colored paper makes good wallpaper, as does wrapping paper. Use a piece of fabric to make carpets and rugs, and don't forget some pictures to go on the walls. Decorate the outside of your house with paint, creating a cheerful summery scene for your doll to live in.

You will need:

Two shoeboxes

Scissors

Tape & glue

Large paper clips

Paint & paintbrushes

Paper & cardboard

Small boxes

Felt-tip pens

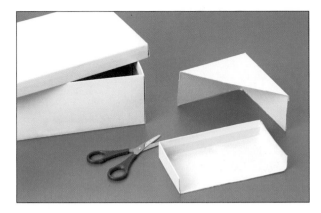

1 Use one of the boxes to make the house. Cut a corner off the other box to make the roof and cut the lid so that it fits inside the house as the upstairs floor.

2 Place the shoe box that will be the house up on one end. Use tape to attach the roof piece you have prepared at an angle to the top of the house. Use glue and tape to stick the floor section into place. Hold the floor in position with the large paperclips while the glue is setting.

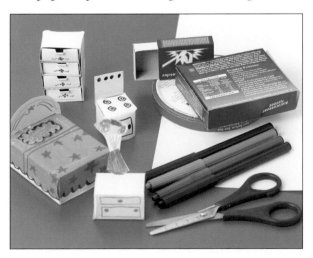

3 When the glue is set your house is ready to decorate. Paint the roof a rich reddy brown and the walls pale pink. Make a front for the house from the other shoe-box lid and cut out windows. Paint a bright front door and flowers and make your house summery and cheerful.

4 Miniature furniture is easy to make from scraps of paper and small boxes. Cover boxes with white paper to make kitchen equipment and colored paper for furniture in other rooms. Use felt-tip pens to outline shapes and decorate the pieces. Don't forget wallpaper and rugs and maybe some pictures on the walls.

SPONGE BOARD
Blow Soccer

Soccer is a very popular sport. Enjoy a game of blow soccer on a rainy day by making your own table-sized soccer field. This field has been made with a piece of sponge board. If you wanted to make a more long-lasting field, you could get an adult to help prepare a piece of chipboard or plywood. You will also need green felt to cover the board, although paint would give a reasonable surface. The game is played using drinking straws and table tennis balls. Each player begins with an equal number of balls and sees how many he or she can blow into the opposite goal. Once you become more professional, you might want to play a more traditional soccer game with one ball decorated using a marker pen to look like a real football.

You will need:
Sponge board

Green felt

Scissors

Glue

Shaped craft strip wood

Paint

Paintbrushes

Cocktail sticks

Colored paper

A shoebox

Drinking straws

Table tennis balls

1 Cut out the felt slightly larger than the board. Spread the board with glue and press the felt onto the board.

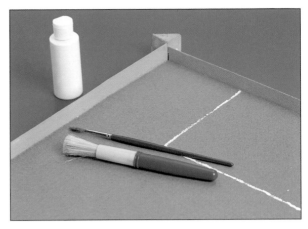

3 Glue the edging in place and use the white paint to mark out the goal mouths and center line.

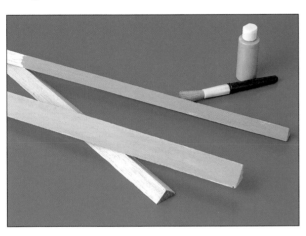

2 Cut the edging to size and paint it yellow. As well as both sides and ends of the pitch, you will need four small pieces to make the corners.

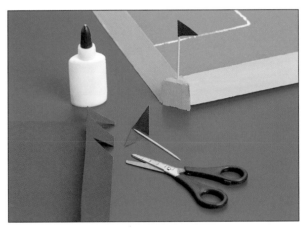

4 Press a cocktail stick into each corner of your field. Fold the colored paper in half and cut out four flag shapes. Glue the flags onto the cocktail sticks.

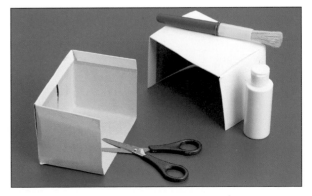

5 Cut the shoebox in half. Paint the halves white and when they are dry place them on the field at opposite goal mouths. Put the table tennis balls in position and it's time to challenge someone to a game!

CARDBOARD
Toy Cars

These cute little cars are great fun to make and given a push will whizz along a smooth surface. The wheels are made from milk or juice container lids, cocktail sticks and straws. The car chassis is cut from either colored cardboard or the sides of a recycled grocery box.

You will need:
Thick cardboard

Scissors

Masking tape

Paint

Paintbrushes

Four juice or milk carton lids

Straws

Cocktail sticks

1 Begin by drawing two side views of a car. Cut them out. Next cut out a long rectangular shape. The width of the rectangle decides how wide the car is.

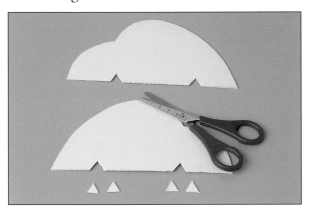

2 Use the scissors to cut out two small v-shapes to form the wheel arches. The wheel axles will run through these v-shapes. The wheel axles will be held in place by the base of the car.

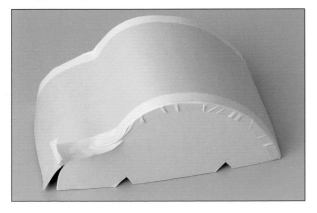

3 Now you are ready to assemble your car. Use masking tape to attach the long rectangular shape to the car sides. Do this and you will see the car take shape.

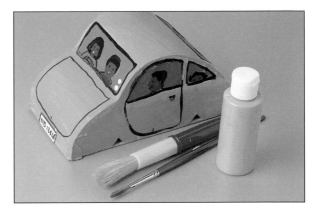

4 Cut a piece of card to fit in the base of the car. Tape it in place. Your car is now ready to paint and decorate. You could paint on a family sitting in the car.

5 To make the wheels each lid will need a hole made through its center. Push the end of a straw through the hole. Now use a cocktail stick to hold it in place. Break the ends off so that the wheel turns.

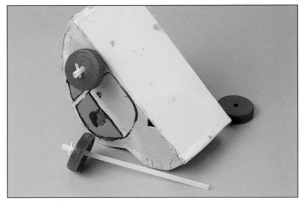

6 Push the wheel axle all the way through and attach the second wheel. Cut off any long pieces of straw to fit the car. Now make and fit the second axle.

Juggling Balls

Juggling is a great skill to develop. It takes time and patience but can be most fulfilling. Make yourself some juggling balls and a set for a friend and practice together. These juggling balls are made from printed cotton fabric and filled with uncooked green lentils. Lentils are a perfect filling as they will give the juggling balls some weight and be easy to grip. They are also quite economically priced—and—if you stop juggling you can cook the lentils for supper!

1 Cut a rectangle of fabric and fold it in half. Sew seams along the side edges. Sew strong stitches close together or ask an adult for help and use a sewing machine.

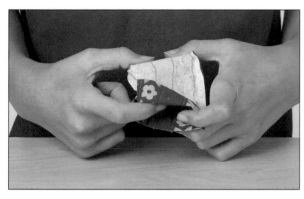

2 Turn the bag shape right side out.

3 Half fill the bags with green lentils.

Juggling balls would make a great birthday gift for a friend.

4 Close the bag making a triangular shape by bringing the two side seam ends together and neatly fold the edges inside to allow for the final seam.

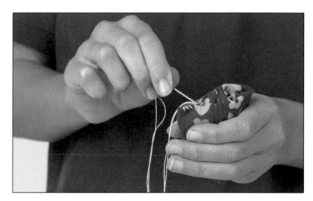

5 Sew the edge together firmly.

You will need:
Fabric

Scissors

Green lentils

Needle and thread

Doll's Bed

You will need a shoebox to make this comfy bed for a doll or teddy bear. The bed is made from the box and the bedhead is made from the lid. The bed will look stylish covered with brightly colored gingham fabric or you could decorate some plain fabric using fabric felt tip pens. Cover the fabric with small flowers or draw out a patchwork spread pattern.

You will need:

A shoebox

Fabric

Scissors

Glue

Lace

Fabric painting pens

Polyester wadding

Needle and thread

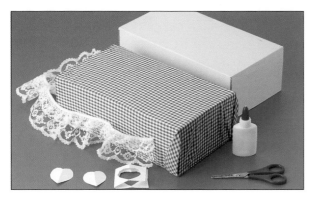

1 Turn the box upside down and cover it neatly with fabric. When attaching fabric it is a good idea to put the glue on the box rather than the fabric. Use a length of gathered lace to create a frill.

4 Gather the fabric into a frill and glue it onto the bed. Make a mattress from polyester wadding and sew on a fabric cover. Decorate the inside of the box lid to make a matching bedhead.

2 Stick a piece of matching fabric onto the inside of the lid of the shoebox to make the bedhead and glue the bedhead onto the base. Cut pieces of polyester wadding to size and sew on fabric covers to make the mattress, pillow and duvet.

5 To make the pillow cut a piece of polyester wadding to a suitable size, fold a piece of fabric over the pillow shape and cut out the cover. Decorate the pillow cover using fabric pens. Use your needle and thread to sew the pillow up.

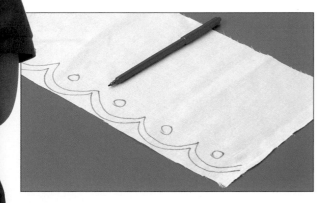

3 The fabric to make this bed is decorated with fabric painting pens. Measure how much fabric you will need to make the frill around the bed. Decorate the frill with a scalloped pattern.

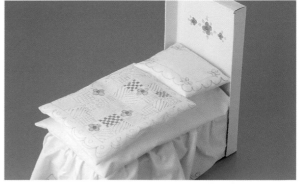

6 Make a duvet from a piece of polyester wadding and fabric. Use fabric pens to decorate the duvet cover so it looks like a patchwork quilt. Copy your scalloped design for the border.

Party Hats

Making party hats is a great way of getting the party spirit going. These hats are quite easy to make from card and crêpe paper, and can be decorated with glitter and junk jewelry.

Try your hand at making a complete set of party hats for a special family meal or celebration. Make Queen and King crowns for the grown-ups and fancy coronets or colorful jester's hats for all the children.

You will need:

Thin cardboard

Scissors

Needle and thread

Crêpe paper

Glue

Glitter

Hair band for the tiara

1 Cut a length of card that will go around your head with a small overlap.

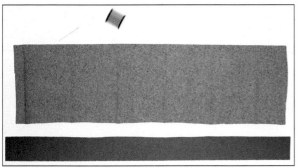

2 Next cut a wide piece of crêpe paper the length of the cardboard. This will need to be quite wide; have a look at the illustration to get an idea of the size. Sew a line of running stitch along one of the long sides of the crêpe paper.

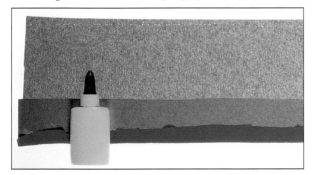

3 Glue the crêpe paper onto the cardboard.

Paint pasta shapes gold or silver and decorate with glitter and use to decorate your crown.

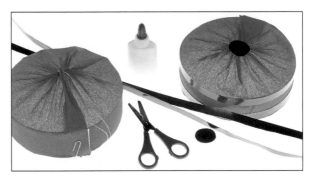

4 Next, glue the paper-covered cardboard into a hat shape. Pull the ends of the thread to gather the crêpe paper and tie a knot. Use crêpe paper to cover a small disk shape of card and glue that over the center of the hat. Decorate the hat with colored paper or card and glitter.

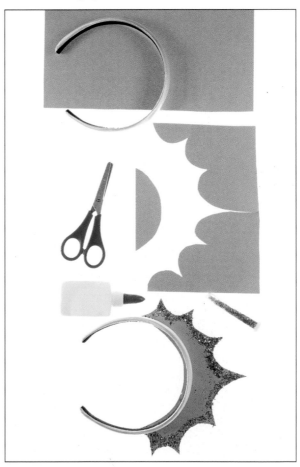

5 This sparkling tiara is made with a hair band and gold card. Lay the hair band onto the card and draw out the shape. Cut out the tiara shape and decorate it with glitter. Attach the tiara to the hair band and leave to dry.

SHOEBOX
Model Theater

Make a model theater and stage your own pageant this Christmas. You will need a shoebox and colored paper to make the theater. Once you have decided on a storyline you can get a script together and decorate sheets of paper to use as scenery.

Make small model trees and furnishings from card and paper. Cut out actors from thin card and use tape to attach them to sticks. You can have as many actors on the stage as you can handle. So you may need a friend or two to help when staging your big production.

You will need:

Shoebox

Scissors

Colored paper

Felt-tip pens and crayons

Glitter

Tape

Thin cardboard

Sticks (kebab sticks would
be the right size
or recycle some
disposable chopsticks)

1 You will need a shoebox to make your theatre. Stand it on its side and cut out an opening on each end. Your actors will enter the stage from these openings.

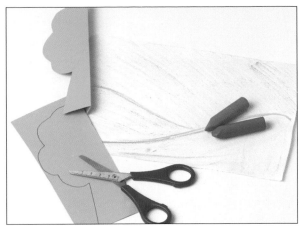

4 Cut a piece of paper to size and decorate it with crayons to make a scene that suits your play. Attach it to the back of the box; this will be your scenery backdrop.

2 Use colored paper to decorate the front of the theater. Make curtains and frills. Use a black felt-tip pen to mark out the gathers. Accentuate the edges with glitter.

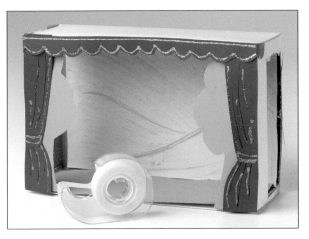

5 Cut out colored paper shapes that match your scenery. Use sticky tape to attach them to the inside edges of the curtains; these are called the wing flats.

3 Glue the curtains into place using sticky tape for difficult corners.

6 Draw your actors onto thin cardboard cut out from the lid of the shoebox. Color them in using felt-tip pens and cut them out. Use tape to attach them to the sticks. Remember they will have to enter the stage through the side entrances, so check for height.

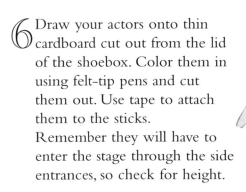

SHOEBOX
Guessing Box

Guessing boxes, filled with interestingly shaped items such as damp squidgy sponges, pine cones or plastic spiders, can be great fun at parties. When players put their hands through the hole their imaginations will turn a damp sponge into something very strange, not the kind of thing one would normally want to touch without looking at it first! Another game to play with a guessing box is to put in a variety of similar things, such as vegetables. Then the players have to guess what they are, by touch.

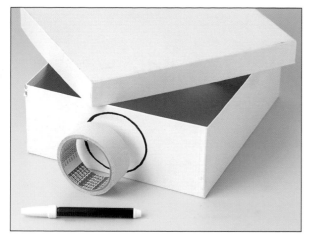

1 Use the circular object to draw a hand-hole on one side of the box.

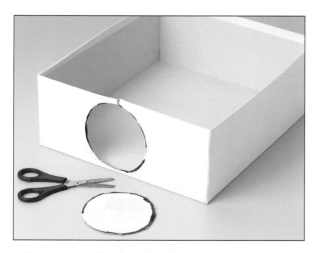

2 Cut out the hand-hole. It is easier to start the hole by cutting down from the top. This cut will be hidden by the lid.

3 Paint the outside of the box and lid black. If necessary, apply two coats.

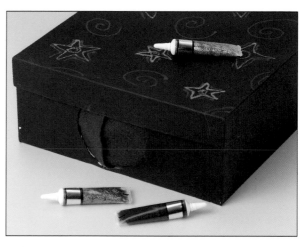

4 Use tape to attach a fabric curtain in the box over the hole and decorate the box with glitter or colored paint.

You will need:

Large shoebox

Circular object to draw around

Pen

Scissors

Paint

Paintbrush

Tape

Piece of fabric

Glitter

FABRIC AND WOOL
Cloth Doll

A soft cloth doll is nice to cuddle up to and looks pretty lying on a pillow as decoration. These dolls are made from cotton fabric and are cut out in a "gingerbread man" shape. Their hair is made from wool and they are dressed in simply shaped clothes tied with ribbon. A cloth doll can be made large, as a bed decoration, or tiny, to live in a dollhouse or be a "pocket" doll. Practice painting faces on a piece of paper to get the shapes right before you paint your doll's face on.

You will need:
Fabric in a flesh color for the doll

Felt-tip pen

Scissors

Needle and thread

Polyester stuffing

Paint

Paintbrush

Wool

Ribbon

Patterned fabric for the doll's dress

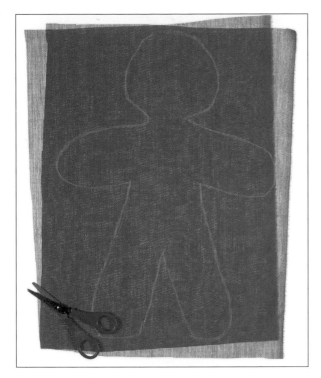

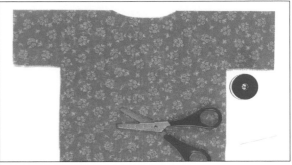

1 Draw a doll shape onto a double layer of fabric. Remember you will need a neck shape that you can sew around and cut out. Look carefully at the picture to get an idea of the shape you need to draw.

3 Use the cut-out doll as a pattern to cut a simple dress shape and sew the edges.

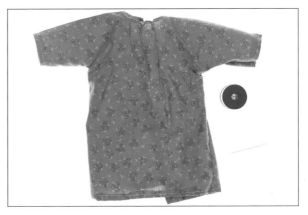

4 Turn the dress the right way out and sew a hem along the bottom of the fabric.

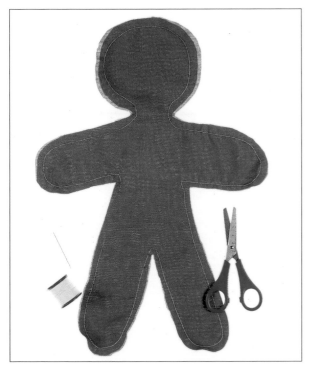

2 Sew around the drawn line, remembering to leave a gap to turn the fabric out. Fill it with stuffing, then cut the doll shape out.

5 Dress your doll and paint on a face. Make hair by winding the wool around a piece of card then sewing a "parting" across the middle. Attach the hair with glue.

6 Tie a ribbon belt in a bow around the waist. Now your doll is ready to enjoy.

Wooden Skewers
Pick-up-Sticks

Pick-up-Sticks is a very old game. Children have played it for generations. To play you need a bundle of similar sized sticks and one pick-up-stick. The player throws the sticks onto the play area and uses the pick-up-stick to help pick up each stick individually without moving any of the others. If the player does nudge another stick her turn is over and the next player gets the sticks to start the process over again. The player who picks up the most sticks is the winner. You can play against yourself by attempting to beat your record each time you play.

1 Divide the skewers into four groups of six with one left over. You will need the felt-tip pens to color the skewers. One skewer will need to be one all over color. This is the stick you will use to help you pick up the others in the game. Choose a different color for each of the four groups of sticks. Color the ends of the sticks with the felt-tip pens.

2 You could make a mini pick-up-sticks set with cocktail sticks!

You will need:
25 wooden skewers
Felt-tip pens

Models and Boxes

Creepy Crawly Pots

Caterpillars, ladybugs, butterflies, and flowers make brilliant decorations on small clay pots. These pots are made from air-hardening clay in the shape of insects and flowers and painted in summer colors. They are great fun to make. Have a look around the garden for creatures to inspire you before you begin.

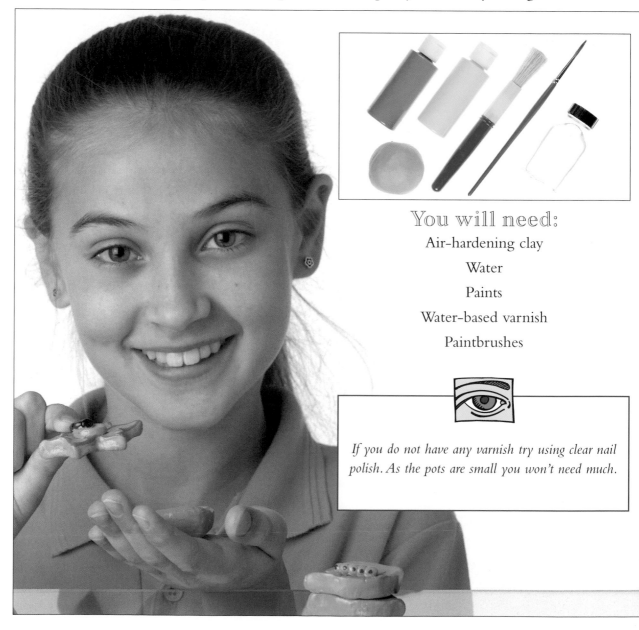

You will need:

Air-hardening clay

Water

Paints

Water-based varnish

Paintbrushes

If you do not have any varnish try using clear nail polish. As the pots are small you won't need much.

1 First make the bowl of the pot, using your thumbs to shape it. Smooth the clay with your finger tips. When you are happy with the shape, make a lid to fit the bowl. Gently stretch the lid into petal shapes and make a little ladybug from two small clay balls. Use a little water to moisten the base of the ladybug before you attach it to the lid. Leave the pot in a warm airy spot to dry. When it is completely dry, paint it, allowing the paint to dry between colors. When the paint is dry, varnish your pot to give it a professional finish.

3 The caterpillar on this pot is made from small balls of clay, all joined up with water. When it is dry, decorate the caterpillar in bright colors.

2 This ladybug pot is very easy to make. Make the base first, using your thumbs to shape it and smooth the clay with your fingertips. Make a lid to fit the base and leave the pot in a warm airy spot to dry. When it is completely dry, paint the inside and outside black. When the black is dry, paint the ladybug red, then paint on the black dots. You may need to touch up the black when it is dry.

Découpage Boxes

Découpage is the art of decorating boxes with paper cutouts. These boxes have been decorated with pictures cut from wrapping paper. Old magazines are a good source for pictures.

Use a box with a tight lid to decorate for a gardening friend to store seeds in, or decorate to hold special handmade decorations for the Christmas tree.

You will need:

Boxes to decorate

Glue

Newspaper

Paint

Paintbrushes

Scissors

Pictures cut from wrapping paper

Water-based varnish

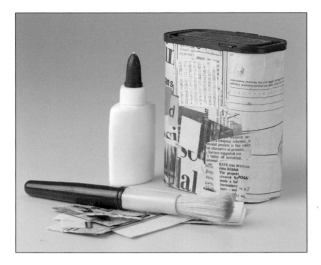

1 Make sure your chosen box is clean inside. Glue on a layer of newspaper squares to cover the box. Leave it in a warm airy spot to dry.

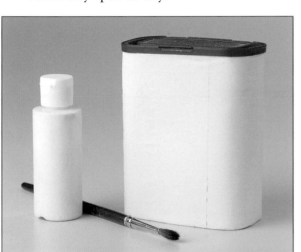

2 When the papier-mâché layer is dry, paint on a base coat of color. You may need two coats to make a good surface to decorate.

3 When the paint is completely dry, the box is ready to decorate. Cut carefully around the pictures, glue on the border and then the feature picture.

4 When the glue is set, the box is ready to varnish. It will need two coats to give it a professional finish.

Decorate small wooden boxes to use for jewelry. Clean up the wood with sandpaper first, then glue on your pictures. Apply two coats of varnish when the glue is dry.

Jewelry Box

Keep your jewelry safe in one of these sparkling treasure troves. The boxes are made from thick card and decorated with gold and silver paint, glitter, glass beads and recycled junk jewelry. If you don't have any suitable old jewels, use brightly decorated gold or silver buttons or sequins.

You will need:

Thick card

Scissors

Sticky tape and glue

Newspaper

Gold paint and glitter

Shiny buttons or jewelry to recycle

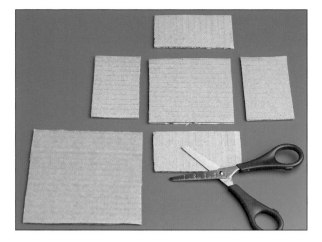

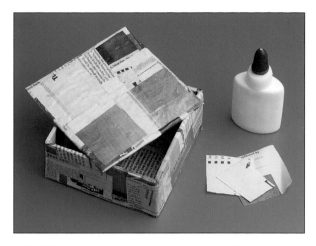

1 Cut a base and lid from thick card. Use the base to measure the size of the walls of the box.

3 Glue two layers of squares cut from the newspaper onto the box and lid. Leave in a warm airy spot to dry.

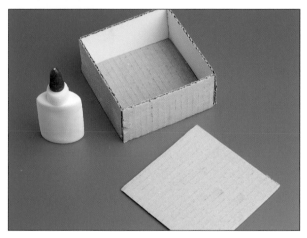

2 Stick the shapes together to form the box. Use glue or tape.

4 When the papier-mâché layer is dry, it is ready to decorate. Paint the box inside and out with gold paint. It may need two coats. When the paint is dry, decorate the lid with glitter, paint, and jewels.

Remember to protect the work surface with newspaper before you begin.

MATCHBOX
Chest of Drawers

The decorations on these tiny chests of drawers give you a good idea of the contents. The chests of drawers are useful for storing stamps or buttons and are made from empty matchboxes, covered with sticky-backed paper. You may want to make a set of drawers for the toolbox to store small nails and screws. The button drawers would be good for saving odd buttons from the sewing box and stamp collectors would find the stamp drawers very useful. You could even make a tiny chest of drawers and decorate it to put in the dollhouse bedroom.

You will need:

Empty matchboxes

Glue

Scissors

Sticky-backed paper

Felt

Selection of buttons and stamps

Thin wire (fuse wire would do well)

Saucer of water

Paper fasteners

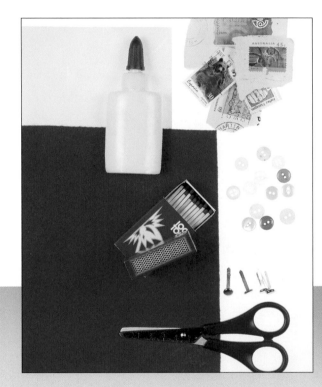

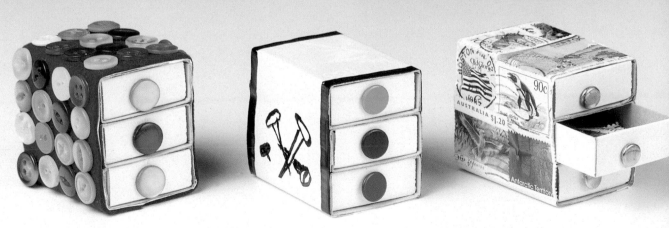

1 To make the button storage drawers, begin by gluing the three matchboxes, one on top of another. When the glue has dried, cover the set of drawers with sticky-backed paper. Spread the box with glue, then stick on the felt covering. Dab on a little glue and stick on the buttons, one at a time. To make handles for the drawers, attach buttons with a little wire.

2 To make the stamp drawer you will need a selection of brightly decorated stamps. Place the stamps in a saucer of water for a few minutes to loosen the glue and remove them from the envelope paper. Glue three matchboxes one on top of another then cover the box with sticky-backed paper. Glue on the stamps, taking care to arrange them so you can see the interesting pictures on them. Make drawer handles from paper fasteners.

You could use stickers to decorate a chest of drawers or decorate the sticky-backed paper with felt-tip pens.

Money Boxes

These stylishly decorated money boxes would look good in the living room. They are made from recycled containers which have good, well-fitting lids. Encourage the whole family to make savings by decorating money boxes for them all. Flowers painted pink, bright orange and yellow, or a money box that suits a particular hobby or style—you can create them easily from old boxes.

You will need:

Sturdy containers with well-fitting lids

Scissors

Newspaper

Glue

Paint

Paintbrushes

1 You will need an adult to help you cut out the money slit. Use a large coin to help measure the space.

3 When the papier-mâché is dry, paint on the base colour, then paint on tiny trees and shrubs.

2 Glue squares of newspaper onto the box to make a good painting surface.

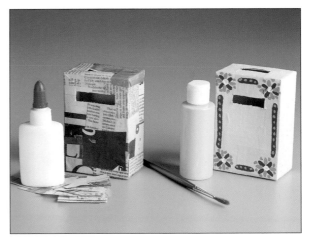

4 These money boxes are made from cardboard boxes. Cut out a slit before covering completely with papier-mâché. Once full they will need to be cut open to get at the money!

FOLDED PAPER
Origami

Paper folding is a useful skill to learn. Follow the instructions and once you have mastered them, if you have a sheet of paper, you will never be without a box. Use stiff cardboard to make a large box and small sheets of paper to make a smaller one. Origami boxes can be used to store party favors, candies, and odds and ends. A sturdy, cardboard–folded box could be used as a simple tray to hold biscuits. Have a go, all you need is a sheet of paper and a little practice.

You will need:
Paper in a selection of colors and weights

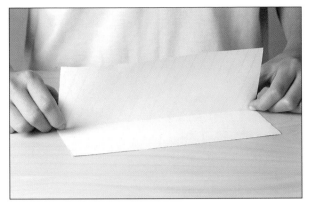

1 Fold the paper in half lengthwise.

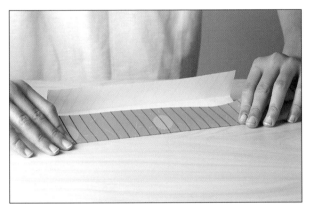

2 Fold each half into the middle.

3 Make a small fold back outward on both sides.

4 Fold in the corners and tuck them under the small fold.

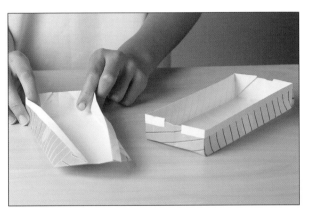

5 Place your fingers in the corners and lift the box into shape.

When paper folding, be sure to press the folds firmly so they are sharp.

CARDBOARD
Pencil Cases

Make yourself a shimmering, space age pencil case with paper, paint, and glitter. Find a container tall enough to carry a ruler and make sure it has a well-fitting lid. An empty spaghetti container or potato chip box could be recycled to make a good pencil case. Once you have glued on a layer of papier mâché your pencil case is ready for decoration. You could create a theme pencil case to match a favourite pen or your book covers and schoolbag.

You will need:
Tall containers with tightly fitting lids

Newspaper

Glue

Scissors

Paint

Paintbrushes

Glitter

1 Clean the container and check that your pens, pencils, and ruler will fit in. Make sure the lid fits well.

Cover the box with a layer of newspaper squares, glued on. Leave in a warm, airy spot to dry.

2 When the papier-mâché layer is completely dry, the pencil case is ready to decorate. Paint it with a base coat then decorate it with space ships, shiny stars and glitter.

Remember to protect your work surface with newspaper before you begin.

When using glitter, place a sheet of paper under your model before sprinkling the glitter. Pour any excess glitter back into the container.

Pencil Tubs

Use paint and glitter to decorate a useful storage tub for pens and pencils. Choose a cylinder-shaped container to recycle into a pencil tub and cover it with a layer of papier-mâché to make it stronger and provide a good surface to decorate.

You will need:

Cardboard containers

Newspaper

Glue

Paint

Glitter

Paintbrushes

Scissors

1 Start by covering the container with a layer of newspaper squares, glued on. Cover the container and leave it in a warm, airy place to dry.

4 When the paint is dry, spread glue on areas you want to glitter and sprinkle on the glitter. Do this one color at a time and leave it to dry between colors.

Before you begin, give the cardboard container a quick wash. Stand it upside down to drain and then dry it with a clean dishtowel.

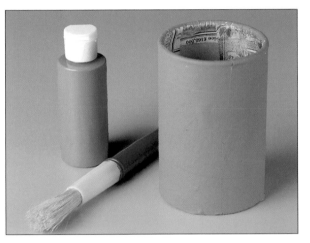

2 When the papier-mâché is completely dry, paint on a base coat and allow it to dry. You may need two coats of paint.

3 Paint on the fish and seaweed, using one color at a time. Don't forget to paint on some air bubbles above the fish.

FABRIC-COVERED
Sewing Box

Keep needles and pins, thread and scissors safely to hand in this pretty, fabric-covered sewing box. The box is made from two layers of thick cardboard, each covered with polyester wadding and fabric, and then glued together. When you have mastered the technique you could make a small travel sewing box to match your home sewing box. A fabric-covered box could also be used to hold handkerchiefs, hairbands, and scrunchies.

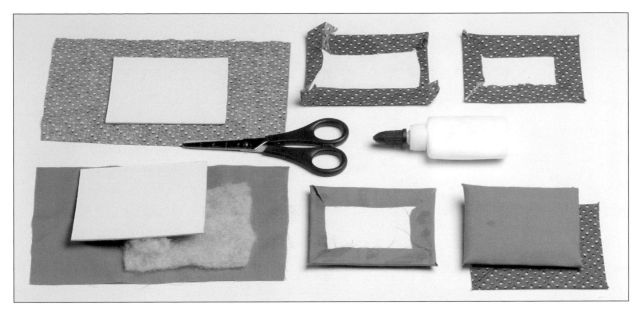

1 Cut the base from thick cardboard. Use this to measure out the sides of the box and cut the lid the same size as the base. This will be the outer box. Cut out two complete sets of cardboard. Now cut one quarter of an inch off around the edge of one set of cardboard pieces. This will be the inner box.

2 Glue a piece of wadding to the four sides of the outer box and cover each one with patterned fabric. Cover the outer lid and base pieces with patterned fabric. Glue a piece of wadding to each piece of the inner box, including the lid and base, then cover these with plain fabric. (Choose co-ordinating fabrics for a stylish effect.)

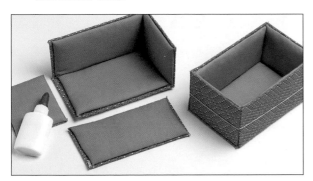

3 Glue the matching outer and inner pieces together. Glue the whole box together and hold it in place with the rubber band.

You will need:

Thick cardboard

Scissors

Wadding

20 inches of patterned fabric

Fabric glue

20 inches of plain fabric

A rubber band

4 To decorate the lid, cover a small square piece of cardboard with plain fabric. Glue this on to the lid. Now cut a strip of fabric, cover it with glue and fold it in half lengthways, roll it up to form a grip, and glue it on to the lid.

Tissue Box Covers

Brighten up a box of tissues with a cover decorated with spring flowers made from colored paper and cardboard. A daffodil-covered tissue box would make a cheery get-well gift for a friend or relative. Once you have mastered the technique you could decorate cardboard with a bunch of daffodils to go with the tissue box. A small posy of colored flowers would look good on a square tissue box.

You will need:

Thick colored cardboard

Scissors

Tape

Colored paper

Glue

1 Use the tissue box as a pattern and cut out the four sides and top of the cover. Ask an adult to cut a wide slit for the tissues to pull through.

4 Shape the fringed strip into the center of the flower by winding it around your finger. Then glue it in place. Check that the pieces form a well-shaped flower.

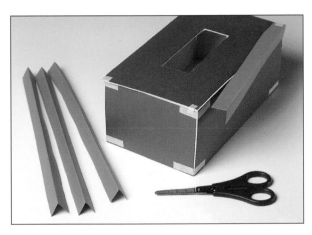

2 Use tape to hold the box together. Cover the tape with decorative edging, cut from colored paper and stuck on with glue.

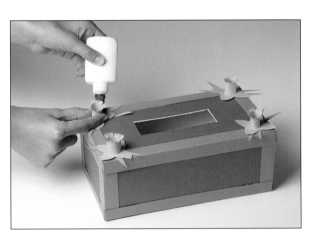

5 Glue the flowers and leaves to your finished tissue box cover. Well done!

3 Cut out the petal shape from yellow paper. Cut out some green leaves. Cut a fringed strip to make the center of the flower.

Cut out and make a few flowers and use the best ones to decorate your tissue box cover. Practice makes perfect!

CARDBOARD
Toy Boxes

Keep your toys and games tidy in one of these stylishly stenciled toy boxes. Use colors and designs that match your bedroom and make stencils easily from sheets of paper. A nicely stenciled toy box would make a good gift for a younger brother or sister, and older family members might like a well-decorated box to use as a storage container.

You will need rather a lot of glue and paint to cover a grocery box. Check with an adult before you begin to make sure you have enough.

1 Cover the grocery box, inside and out, with two layers of newspaper, glued on. Do this in stages, allowing the box to dry in a warm, airy place between layers.

3 Draw your stencil design onto the center of a sheet of paper and cut it out carefully. You may want to make a few stencils and try them out on scrap paper.

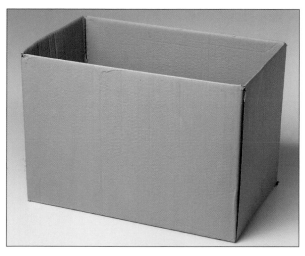

2 When the papier mâché layer is dry, paint the box. Sometimes a second coat of paint is needed to cover the newspaper. Let the paint dry between coats.

4 Hold the stencil on the box. Dip the sponge into a little paint and pat it on the saucer. Practice on scrap paper before decorating your toy box.

You will need:

Grocery box

Glue

Newspaper

Paint

Paintbrushes

Paper

Scissors

Sponge

Saucer

Wastebaskets

L et these brightly colored wastebaskets inspire you to make a tidy version for every room in the house. The wastebaskets are made from cardboard and easily decorated with wrapping paper for a very stylish finish. Big sister will like the gold-colored bin and the floral one will look good in the bathroom. The dotty wastebasket will brighten the hall and I'm sure you know someone who would love a dinosaur-covered bin.

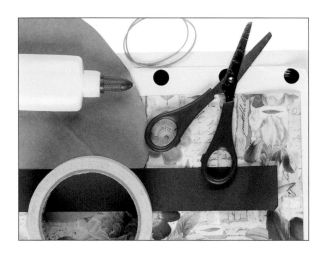

You will need:
Pencil

Thick cardboard

Scissors

Stiff cardboard

Rubber band

Glue

Masking tape

Wrapping paper

Colored paper

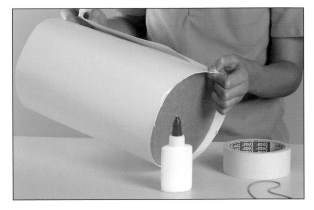

1 Begin by making the base of the box. Draw an oval shape onto thick cardboard (recycled cardboard from a grocery box would be good) and cut it out.

3 Put some glue around the edge of the base. Cut a piece of masking tape the height of the rim and attach it to one side of the wall of the basket.

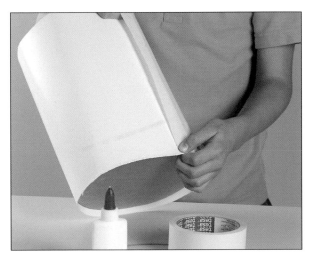

2 Cut out the wall of the basket from stiff cardboard. Use the base to measure how long it should be. Shape it into a cylinder and hold it in place with the rubber band.

4 Wind the wall around the base and hold it in place with the masking tape.

5 Your basket is now ready to decorate with wrapping paper or dinosaur cutouts.

Woodland Cottage

This little log cottage is just waiting for someone to visit and enjoy the pastries and apples set out on the table. The cottage is made from a grocery box and corrugated cardboard. The flowers on the front of the cottage are made from scrunched-up scraps of tissue paper, glued directly on to the walls. When you have made the model, you might try your hand at making some furnishings to put inside the woodland cottage.

You will need:

Corrugated and thick card

Tape

Scissors

Glue

Newspaper

Paint and paintbrushes

Colored tissue paper

Some plastic potted plants

Oven-bake clay

Small rolling pin

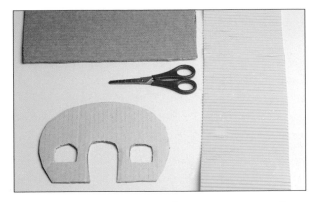

1 Decide on the size of your cottage and cut out the base from thick cardboard. Next cut out a front for the cottage. Ask an adult to help if you have difficulty. Cut out the windows and door. Use a wide strip of corrugated cardboard to shape the rest of the cottage.

4 Paint the house, allowing each color to dry before you start on the next one. Use crumpled-up pieces of tissue paper to decorate the house, choosing different colors for the various flowers, and green for leaves. A few plastic plants will give your woodland cottage a realistic feel.

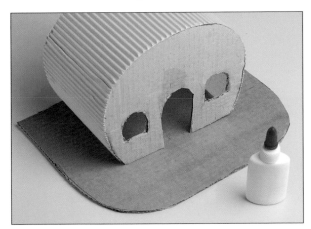

2 Tape the cottage into shape. You may need a little help, one pair of hands to hold things and another pair to attach the tape.

5 The furnishings are made from oven-bake clay. Roll it out on a clean surface and shape the log-style bench and table. Make some tiny pastries to put on the table.

3 Cover the entire model with two layers of newspaper squares, glued on. Leave it in a warm airy place until it is dry.

If you don't have any oven-bake clay, use Plasticine to make the furnishings and food.

CARDBOARD
Trinket Boxes

Boxes are great fun to make. These are painted and decorated with glass beads, paints, and glitter. Make a box to store your earrings, rings, and other small treasures. The square and rectangular boxes are made from recycled grocery box cardboard and the heart-shaped and oval boxes are made from corrugated cardboard. You can sometimes find this as packing or it can be bought in bright colors from a craft shop. The decoration on your box could give a clue as to what is inside it!

You will need:
Thick cardboard

Scissors

Tape

Newspaper

Glue

Paint

Paintbrushes

Corrugated cardboard

Tissue paper

Glitter or glass beads

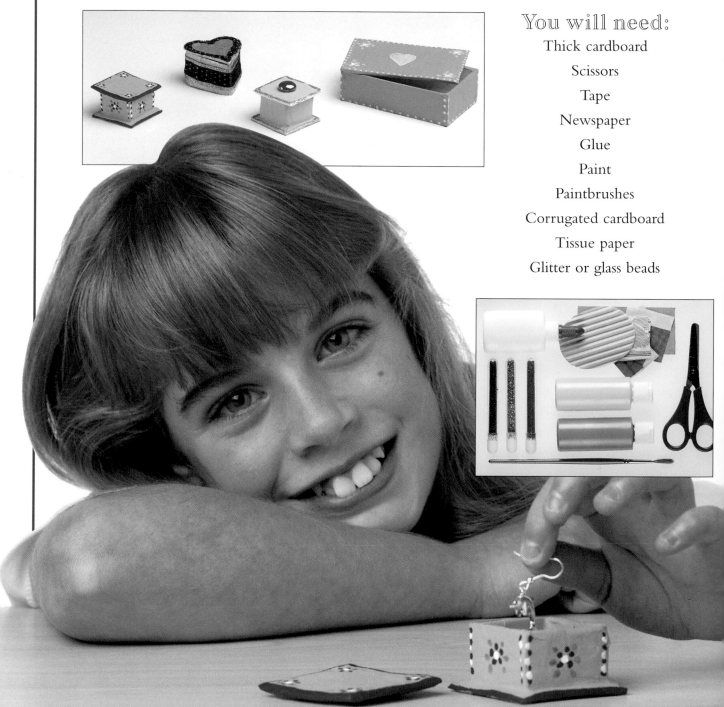

1 Use cardboard from a grocery box. Decide on the size of your box, then measure out a base and sides. The lid is made from two squares of cardboard, one smaller than the other.

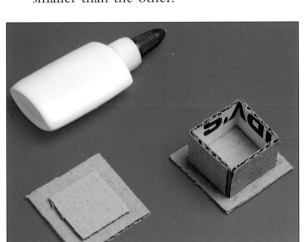

2 Use tape to hold the box together and make sure the lid fits. It will need to be the same size as the base, and the smaller piece of cardboard will need to fit into the box.

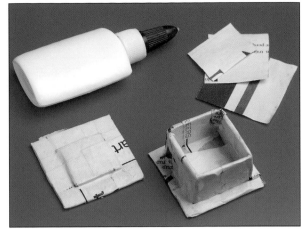

3 Cover the box with a layer of papier-mâché made from newspaper squares, glued on. Check the lid fits and then leave the box and lid in a warm airy spot to dry before you begin to decorate it with paint.

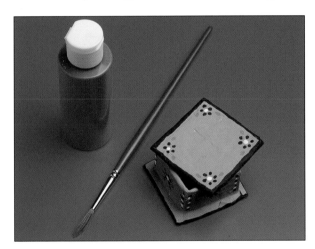

4 When the papier-mâché is dry, paint a base coat of color. You may need to give the box a second coat of paint. Use the point of the brush to paint flowers and leaves on the box and lid, and paint a bright red border.

5 This oval box is made from corrugated cardboard which is easy to bend. Cut an oval shape for the base. The lid will need to be larger than the base, so it fits over the side. This box is covered with colored tissue paper. Decorate the edge of a heart-shaped box with glitter or glass beads.

Desk Tidies

Use brightly colored thin cardboard triangles to make these desk tidies, and put them to good use holding odd paperclips or erasers. They are held together with strips of tape. The containers have a simple design and their stylish shape and bright colors means they can be left plain or decorated with felt-tip pens or brightly colored strips of tape.

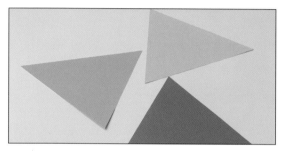

1 Begin with a triangular sheet of of thin cardboard. You will need to repeat the instruction at each corner.

3 Make a second fold by folding the corner back on itself. Press firmly along the fold.

2 Fold the first corner over to the opposite straight edge and press firmly along the fold.

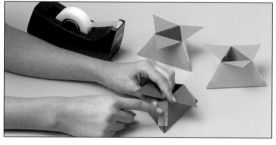

4 When all the sides are folded, use tape along the corners to hold the containers in shape.

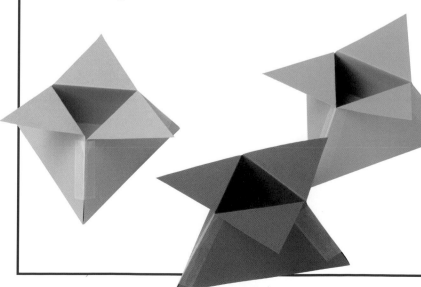

You will need:
Thin cardboard triangles
Tape

Special Occasions

PAPER DRAGON
Chinese New Year

The Chinese New Year is a time when families enjoy reunions and gifts, as with so many of the winter festivals. The story goes that once there was a bad dragon who terrorized the people. The people were very frightened but after a while they discovered that the dragon didn't like loud noises, so they all got together and made lots of loud noises. They banged saucepan lids together, shouted and let off firecrackers to frighten him away. Nowadays there is a grand dragon procession with fireworks and many people holding up a giant paper dragon. After the event families join together to eat specially prepared meals to welcome in the New Year. They give gifts of money wrapped in red envelopes to each other. The Chinese New Year begins with a new moon, and it is also the time when the farmers gave thanks for the harvest. Have fun making your own small Chinese dragon and if there are a few of you, why not make lots of dragons so you can have your own Chinese New Year procession.

You will need:
Thin cardboard

Felt-tip pens

Glitter

Glue

Scissors

Tissue paper

Paper

Tape

Two sticks

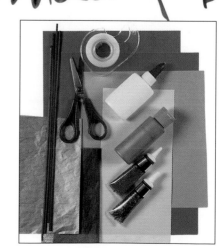

1 Draw a dragon's head onto a piece of thin cardboard. Use felt-tip pens to color and decorate it with glitter.

4 Make the body by taking two strips of paper and folding them one over the other repeatedly to make a concertina.

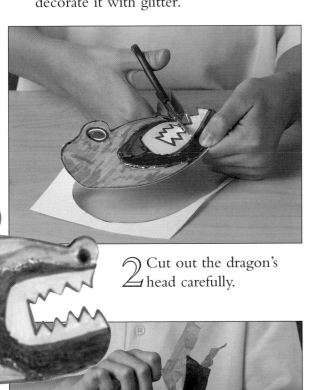

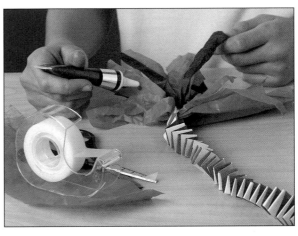

2 Cut out the dragon's head carefully.

5 Attach paper ribbons to the dragon's tail. Glue the head to the other end of the body.

3 Cut strips of tissue paper to use as ribbons. Use the glue to stick these paper ribbons to the dragon's head.

6 Use sticky tape to attach the sticks to the dragon's body. One is for the head and the other for the tail.

St. Valentine's Day

You will need a heart shaped cookie cutter to make both the picture frames and the gingerbread hearts! Both will make great Valentine gifts to give to friends and sweethearts. The gingerbread cookies are simple to make and can be decorated with frosting or left plain. Either way they are delicious to eat. The heart shaped picture frame has space for two pictures. It is made by rolling out the clay and using two cookie cutters to cut the frame, one smaller than the other. A coat of varnish (or clear nail polish) will give your picture frame a professional finish.

You will need:

Air hardening clay

Heart cookie cutter

Red paint

Paint-brush

Thread or ribbon

Glue

Recipe for gingerbread cookies

2 1/3 cups plain flour

1 teaspoon baking powder

2 teaspoons ground ginger

1 teaspoon cinnamon

1 stick margarine

1 cup soft brown sugar

3 tablespoons syrup

1 egg

Frosting

1 Place the flour, baking powder, ginger, cinnamon, and sugar in a large bowl. Add the margarine, mix it in well with your fingertips until the mixture looks crumbly like breadcrumbs.

2 Add the sugar and syrup; mix together. Use a spoon to stir in the egg and mix.

3 Turn the mixture out onto the work surface and knead the mixture until it is smooth and well mixed. Sprinkle some flour onto the work surface and use the rolling pin to roll the mixture out to a thickness of about one quarter of an inch. With a heart-shaped biscuit cutter cut out the shapes. Place the shapes on a baking tray and bake at 325°F for just 10 minutes. Get an adult to help you use the oven.

4 When the gingerbread biscuits are cooked take them out of the oven and leave to stand until cold. They will harden up as they cool. When they are cool, decorate the cookies with frosting.

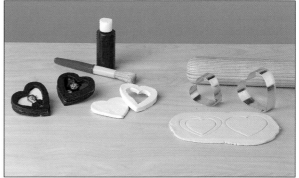

5 To make these picture frames you will need two cookie cutters, one smaller than the other, and some air-hardening clay. Roll out the clay and cut out two large heart shapes. One of the heart shapes will be the picture frame back. Take the smaller heart-shaped cookie cutter and cut a small heart shape out of the second heart shape. Leave the made frame pieces to dry in a warm airy place. When they have dried completely, paint them with red paint and glue them together. Place a picture of your Valentine in the frame. Use glue to secure it to the frame.

The heart-shaped frames look good enough to eat, but remember they are made from air-hardening clay and are not edible!

Mother's Day

Make your mother this pretty photo wallet for Mother's Day. It is made with card and attractive handmade paper, but would be equally good made with decorated paper or covered with a printed fabric. A photograph of you when you were a baby would make a good cover picture rather than the cut-out flower. If you have brothers and sisters put photographs of all of you in the wallet. Use your imagination and the materials you have in your scrap box to come up with something good.

You will need:

Scissors

Paper

Cardboard

Glue

Ribbon

Pictures

Photographs

1 You will need two equal sized pieces of thick cardboard for the cover. Glue them onto attractive handmade paper.

4 Glue a piece of ribbon to the inside of both cardboard covers. This will tie in a pretty bow to keep your wallet closed.

2 Fold the handmade paper in neatly and firmly, then glue it securely down, so that the outer edges of the two pieces of cardboard are completely covered.

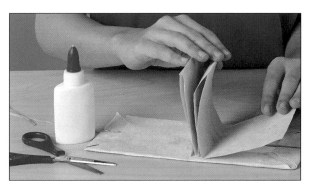

5 Stick one end of the folded page section to the inside front cover. It should cover the ribbon end too. Fix the other end of the page section to the inside back cover.

3 Now take a long piece of handmade paper and make a concertina fold. This will make the pages of the wallet.

6 Decorate the front cover with ribbon and a cutout picture of flowers, or maybe use a picture of yourself.

GIFTS, CARDS, AND DECORATIONS
Easter

In the Northern Hemisphere Easter occurs in the springtime, so we have Easter bunnies, eggs, and spring flowers, such as the daffodils on this delightful Easter card. It is fun to make and grandparents will enjoy receiving greeting cards at this time of year. The chocolate nests are made from breakfast cereal and melted chocolate. The tiny eggs are chocolate covered raisins, or, instead, you could use small foil covered chocolate Easter eggs. Another fun Easter activity is to make an Easter tree. This tree is made from a branch decorated with paper Easter eggs.

You will need:

Shredded breakfast cereal

Bowl

Melted chocolate

Spoon

Foil

Muffin pan

Chocolate covered raisins

1 Crumble the cereal by hand into a bowl. Check that there are no large chunks.

2 Carefully add the melted chocolate to the bowl of crumbled cereal and, using the spoon, mix well together.

3 Line a muffin pan with foil and place a spoonful of the mixture into each space. Use the back of the spoon to press it down into a nest shape. Leave the shapes to harden in a cool, dry place.

4 When the nests are hard, put them on a plate and add a few chocolate covered raisins to each one. Serve up as a treat on Easter Sunday.

5 A branch decorated with paper Easter eggs will brighten up the home. Cut the Easter eggs from paper and decorate them using pencil crayons. Make a hole at one end of each egg and thread with string to hang them on the Easter tree.

6 Use colored paper to make this Easter card. The daffodils have bright yellow paper petals and a paler yellow center. Cut the leaves from green paper. Use glue to attach the flowers to the card.

Father's Day

This useful paperweight should be a great success as a gift on Father's Day. You will need a wooden doorknob or other small, but weighty, object to decorate. Choose a decoration that will suit his personality or hobbies; a garden-loving father would enjoy the gardening design and a handyman would like the woodworking tools! If he plays golf you could stick a real golf ball and tee onto the paperweight. Paint the paperweight in colors that suit the decoration—greens and browns for gardening or maybe blue, if your decoration has a watery theme.

You will need:

Wooden doorknob

Oven-bake clay

Glue

Paintbrush

Paint

Varnish

Small decorations could be made from air-hardening clay and painted if you did not have any oven-bake clay.

1 Use colored oven-bake clay to make the vegetables. The carrots are made from tiny sausage shapes thinned at one end with a few green pieces stuck on as stalks. To make the cabbages begin with a few small ball shapes, and flatten them into leaf shapes. When you have made a few leaves press them, one by one, onto a small ball, until you have a hearty-looking cabbage. Pumpkins are made from flattened ball shapes, and the tomatoes are small red ball shapes with tiny green stalks. The miniature basket came from a florist's shop, but you could make a basket from clay. Harden the vegetables in the oven according to the manufacturer's instructions. Paint the doorknob dark green. Use strong glue to attach the vegetables and basket to the doorknob.

3 The doorknob has been left unpainted for this carpenter's design. Make the miniature tools from oven-bake clay, baked in the oven according to the manufacturer's instructions.

4 Use glue to attach the hardened tools to the doorknob and when the glue has dried, varnish the paperweight. For a golfing father, decorate the doorknob with a golf ball and tee.

2 When the glue has dried brighten up the paperweight with a little red paint and then varnish the whole item to give a professional finish.

Harvest Supper

Harvest is a special time of year. It comes at the end of summer when the farmers have harvested all the summer grown crops, ready to store for winter use. After harvest, wheat is ground into flour for bread and the kitchens of vegetable gardeners are full to overflowing. We have prepared a pot of soup using a mixture of seasonal vegetables and made some bread rolls and a loaf to enjoy with the soup. Ask an adult to supervise the cooking and make a special family harvest supper.

You will need:

A package bread mix

Bowl

A little extra flour

Baking tray

Egg

Pastry brush

Rack

Soup ingredients

Knife

Large saucepan and water

Fork

Small soup bowl

Soup recipe:

1 onion

2 sticks of celery

2 medium potatoes

2 large carrots

1 leek

A vegetable stock cube

1 teaspoon of mixed herbs

A squeeze of tomato paste

A little oil

Salt and pepper to taste

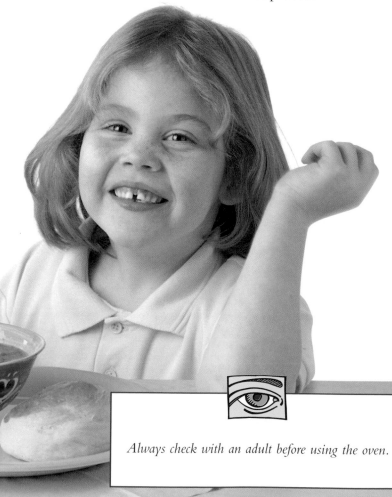

Always check with an adult before using the oven.

1 Follow the directions on the bread mix package. You will need to pour the package mix into a bowl and add the required quantity of water. Mix well with a spoon until the mixture forms a dough.

2 Sprinkle the work surface with a little flour. Empty the dough onto the work surface and use your hands to knead it. After a few minutes you will see and feel that the dough becomes smooth. When it is all smooth to touch and eye, you can begin to shape it.

3 Divide it in two sections and shape it into bread rolls and a plaited loaf. Place them on a baking tray. Brush with beaten egg and leave in a warm spot to rise. When the dough has doubled in size, bake according to the instructions on the package.

4 When the bread is ready it will smell delicious and be a lovely golden brown color. Ask an adult to help take the bread out of the oven. Place the cooked bread on a rack to cool.

5 Chop up the vegetables before you begin to make the soup. Place all the ingredients into a large saucepan. Pour enough water into the saucepan to cover the ingredients. Bring to the boil and then turn down the heat so the soup cooks gently. Allow to cook for half an hour.

6 Ask an adult to help. Prick some of the vegetables with a fork to make sure they are cooked. Season with salt and pepper if necessary. Serve in a small soup bowl and enjoy your soup with your freshly baked harvest bread and rolls.

SAND AND PETAL PICTURE
Diwali

Followers of the Hindu religion celebrate many festivals. Diwali, or the Festival of Light, is my favorite Hindu festival. Diwali is celebrated around October/November time and is a New Year celebration. In Hindu homes the house is cleaned and decorated with colored glitter, sand, and flowers. Lots of small clay lamps are kept burning on windowsills and on doorsteps. These lights are to welcome Lakshmi, the goddess of wealth. Everyone hopes she will visit them over this period and bring good fortune for the New Year. Many Hindu homes in India have sand pictures drawn up outside their front doors to welcome visitors. Make a sand and flower picture to place in your hall during Diwali.

You will need:
Air-hardening clay

Paintbrush and paint

Paper and pencil

Glue stick

Colored sand

Flower petals

Glitter

Before you use a candle make sure you have an adult present.

232

1 To make your Diwali lamp you will need a ball of air-hardening clay. Use your fingers to shape it into a bowl shape and press a fancy edge into the clay. When the lamp has dried, paint it in bright colors and decorate with gold or silver paint. Place a nightlight candle in the lamp and check with an adult before you light it.

2 You will need a large piece of paper. Use a pencil to sketch a flower picture onto the paper. Use a glue stick to mark the centre of the flower.

3 Pour colored sand onto the glue mark.

4 Next use the glue stick to mark out the shape of the petals.

5 Pour colored sand onto the glue lines.

6 When you have completed the sand picture place flower petals as a border.

7 Use glitter to add the finishing touch to your Diwali picture.

Halloween

Halloween is a spooky time of year. Make a hollowed-out pumpkin lantern. Carve a face on one side of the pumpkin and stand it outside your home with a lit candle inside. The golden candle light will shine through the dark! For ghoulish fun try making this very squidgy Halloween game. Your friends will enjoy plenty of laughs searching the green gunge for spiders and worms. The glow-in-the-dark character worm is made from oven-bake glow clay. You could make some to put in trick or treat boxes. Open them in the dark to enjoy the glow!

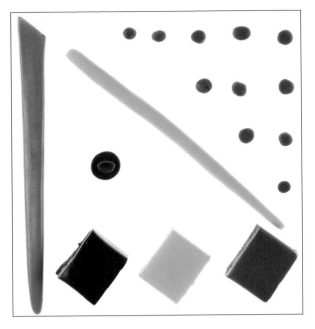

1 Half fill a large bowl with water. Add enough food coloring to turn the water dark green. Sprinkle 3 or 4 tablespoons of wallpaper glue onto the water. Allow the wallpaper glue to sink to the bottom and then stir gently with the spoon until the mixture is sloppy and thick.

2 Add the spiders and toads and the game is ready to play. Take turns to feel through the gunge and guess which creature you are fishing out.

3 Make the cute little glow-in-the-dark worm with special oven-bake glow clay. Make the body first, then form it into the worm shape. Make a number of small ball shapes in dark green and flatten them. Press them onto the worm. Make a hat and place it on the worm's head. Bake the completed model according to the manufacturer's instructions. You could stand the finished worm on a shelf as an ornament or turn him into a fridge magnet or brooch.

You will need:

Bowl

Water

Green food coloring

Wallpaper glue

A selection of plastic toads and spiders

Oven-bake glow clay

Pumpkin

Knife

Candle

FESTIVAL CANDLESTICK
Hanukkah

Hanukkah is the Jewish festival of lights. It is celebrated as a reminder of the time 2,000 years ago when the Jewish Temple was destroyed in battle by the Syrian king. When the battle was over the Jewish people repaired the Temple and went to light the oil lamp which burns in front of the Ark. They found they had hardly any oil, only enough for one day. But, by a miracle, the oil lasted eight days, long enough for the people to prepare more Holy oil to burn. Nowadays Jewish families celebrate Hanukkah in December for eight days, lighting a candle each day until they are all lit. Then they enjoy a time of celebration with parties, games and gifts. You can make a small Hanukkah candlestick to stand on a windowsill. Keep it lit through the festival.

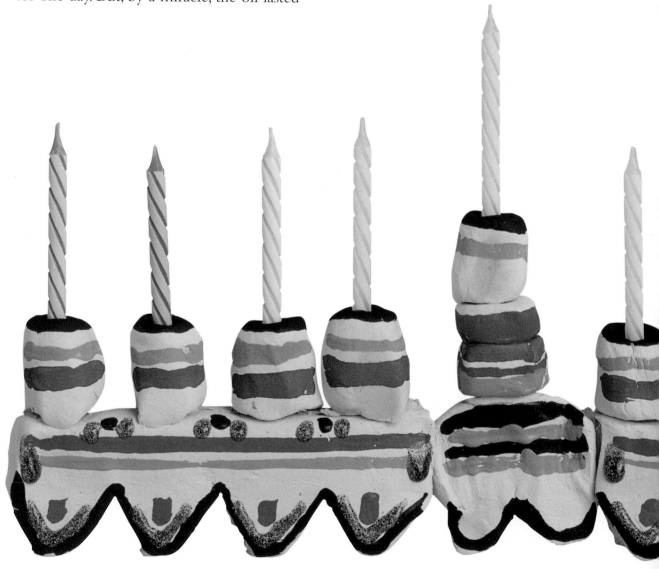

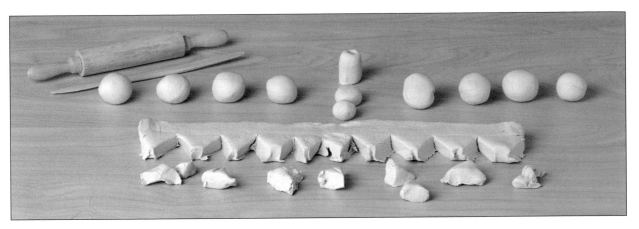

1 Divide your clay into thirds. Roll two thirds out into a long rectangle. Cut out a zig-zag pattern to make the base of the candlestick. Flatten the edges of the zig-zag so that the candlestick will stand securely. The remaining third of the clay will make the candleholders. You will need one candleholder in the center and four on each side of it.

2 Assemble the candlestick and leave it in a dry, warm, airy place before decorating it.

3 The candlestick is decorated with paint and glitter. Ask an adult to help each day. First light the center candle and use that to light the other candles day by day. On the first day light one candle, on the second light two candles and so on, until the eighth when all eight candles will be lit.

You will need:

Air-hardening clay

Modeling tool

Paint

Paintbrush

Glitter

Candles

Advent

Τhe twenty-four days before Christmas are marked by an Advent calendar. This calendar is made from a sheet of painted chipboard. Hammer twenty-four tacks into the decorated board and on each tack hang a small gift. You can fill small boxes with a mixture of homemade gifts and bought trinkets. Chocolate or other candies would be suitable Advent gifts to wrap and hang up on the calendar. You might want to make an Advent calendar for a younger brother or sister to hang in their own room as sharing the treats may be difficult!

1 Paint one side of the chipboard a rich dark blue. It may need more than one coat.

4 Hammer twenty-four tacks into the board. Space them out evenly.

2 Use a sponge dipped in silver paint to decorate the edges of the board.

5 Use brightly colored tissue paper and gold thread to wrap up all twenty-four small gifts you have collected. Hang the gifts up on the board and your Advent calendar is ready to use.

3 Cut a star shape from the center of a piece of paper and use it as a stencil. Use the sponge and silver paint to stencil stars attractively across the blue painted board.

You will need:

Piece of chipboard

Paint and paintbrush

Sponge and saucer

Paper

Scissors

Hammer and 24 tacks

Small gifts

Tissue paper

Gold thread

Christmas Time

When the Christmas tree goes up we know Christmas is definitely on the way. Presents will soon be piling up underneath it and excitement is in the air. Spend an afternoon making some of these decorations to hang on your tree. You can use card and paper, glitter and string to make these keepsake decorations. The tiny angels are made from rice and pasta shapes, glued together and painted gold. They are quite easy for even tiny hands to make.

You will need:

Dried pasta quill and bow shapes

Glue

Small wooden balls or beads to use as angel heads

Rice

Gold thread

Gold paint and paintbrush

Paper or gold tissue paper

Poppy seedpods

Thin metallic cardboard

Glitter

If you do not have glitter glue, make your own. Use strong white glue and mix in an equal amount of fine glitter.

1 Use strong glue to stick the pasta shapes together. Begin with a quill shape, this will be the angel body. A bow shape will make the angel wings, glue this onto the quill. Glue a wooden ball on as a head and a few grains of rice as hair, and a loop of thread to hang the angel onto the tree. When the glue has dried firmly, decorate the angel with gold paint.

3 Save some poppy seedpods in the summer. Dry them and when Christmas comes round turn them into beautiful baubles. Cut away the stems and glue on a loop of gold thread to hang the decoration onto the tree. Paint the seedhead gold and when dry you will have a lovely tree decoration.

2 This shower of gold stars looks very pretty hanging on the Christmas tree. Cut star shapes from gold tissue paper or plain paper painted gold. Glue the stars onto long pieces of gold thread and then drape them over the Christmas tree. These stars would also look good draped across the mantlepiece, shimmering in the light.

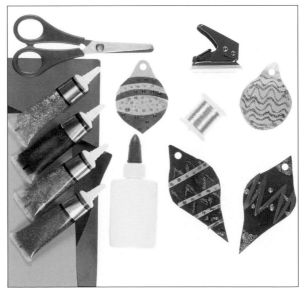

4 These colorful baubles are cut out of thin metallic cardboard. Use a paper punch to make a hole for the loop of thread and decorate the baubles with strips of metallic cardboard and glitter.

NATIVITY SCENE
Christmas Eve

A small Nativity scene looks beautiful set up on the mantlepiece at Christmas time and reminds us of the wonderful story of Jesus' birth. This miniature scene is made from air-hardening clay. The shapes are all very simple and each piece is painted carefully to create the characters. The stable is made from clay but you might want to decorate a small box as the stable and then use the box to store the Nativity scene when not on display. A Nativity scene would make a thoughtful gift for grandparents. You could keep it to use again next year.

You will need:

Air-hardening clay

Paint

Paintbrushes

Gold glitter

Varnish

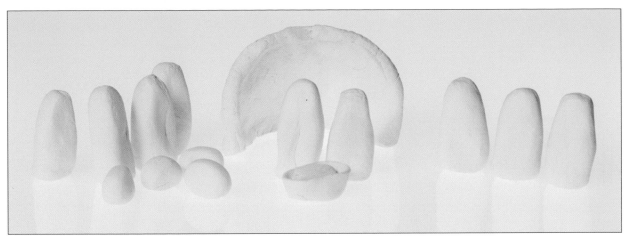

1 Begin by shaping the stable from a ball of clay. Next make a small cradle to hold Baby Jesus. Make a small baby shape and place it in the cradle. Mary and Joseph will be next; make Joseph a little larger than Mary. You will need a few shepherds and some shapes for sheep. Make sure these will stand up on their own. Make the three wise men last. Leave all the clay pieces to dry in a warm airy spot, then you can decorate them.

2 Follow the illustration above when painting your Nativity scene. Mary will need to have a blue cloak, and the three wise men should have a bit of gold glitter sparkling on them somewhere. Paint the sheep white with black faces and legs. When the scene is all painted allow the pieces to dry, then varnish them.

3 Joseph, Mary, and Baby Jesus in the manger: a Christmas scene to remind us of the real reason behind Christmas.

CRACKERS

Christmas Day

Home made Christmas crackers are one of the many things you can make in advance in preparation for Christmas. Fill them with paper hats, jokes (good ones!) and small gifts which you could make, such as necklaces or small brooches or badges. Paper hats are easy to make from tissue paper. You will need to fold them up small so they fit in the crackers. The snaps are available from craft shops. You might want to make a special cracker for a grandparent or friend you won't be seeing over the Christmas season. Send it to them through the post so that they can pull it while they are enjoying their Christmas dinner.

You will need:

Tissue paper, for hat and cracker

Scissors

Thin cardboard

Sticky tape

Small gift to put inside the cracker

Snaps

Glue

Glitter

You could use the central cardboard cylinder from a roll of toilet paper to shape your crackers.

1 Before you make the cracker you will need to make a tissue paper hat. Use your own head to make a standard size hat. If you are making the hat to fit an adult-head, make it a little larger. Cut a zigzag shape along one side, and glue the two short edges together.

2 To make the cracker you will need a sheet of tissue paper measuring 16 in. x 8 in. and three pieces of thin cardboard 7 in. x 4 in. Add a snap, a paper hat tightly folded, and a small gift.

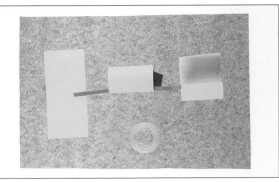

3 Roll the pieces of thin cardboard into cylinder shapes. Hold them in place with tape. Run the snap through the cylinders and place the hat and gift in the central cylinder.

4 Roll the tissue paper around the cylinders and use thread to tie in between them. Pull up the thread firmly to create the cracker shape. Remove the two end cylinders and trim any excess paper away.

5 The cracker is ready to decorate. Use glitter and glue on a seasonal picture.

CAKES
Special Days

These novelty cakes look great on a party table and would make a surprise birthday gift to take to a party. The frosting is simply rolled out with a rolling pin then placed over the cake. The decorative pieces are cut using cookie cutters which come in so many shapes and sizes you are sure to find one to suit the style of cake you want to make. Use a bought-in sponge cake to frost or make your own. Ask an adult for help when you use the oven.

1 Sieve some superfine sugar onto your work surface so that the frosting doesn't stick to it and roll out the frosting to about a quarter inch thickness.

2 Roll the frosting over the rolling pin and, lifting it gently, transfer it to the cake. Drape it over the cake and carefully remove the rolling pin.

3 Gently press the frosting over the cake. Cut away any excess frosting with a knife. Use a clean cloth to wipe away any frosting sugar.

4 Roll out some red frosting and use a cookie cutter to cut out the star shapes. Moisten the back of the stars with water and press them gently onto the cake.

5 Use different shaped cookie cutters to create different styles of cake. Green frogs, red stars, or blue fish could be cut out and decorated further with silver balls or edible felt-tip colors. Have fun creating your own designs to suit different occasions.

You will need
Sponge cakes to frost

Superfine sugar

Rolling pin

Easy-roll frosting

Knife

Clean cloth

Small sieve

Cookie cutters

A little water and a pastry brush

OVEN–BAKE CLAY
Thanksgiving

Thanksgiving is a special festival that has been celebrated every year in the United States of America since about 1620. The Pilgrim settlers who sailed across the Atlantic ocean in wooden sailing ships, arrived in America and established their colony in 1620. Their first winter was hard and they had very little to eat and many of them died from sickness. In the spring the friendly Native American people brought them food and taught them which herbs and plants were good as medicine and food. The Native Americans helped the settlers plant crops of corn and other vegetables which grew well in America. When the crops were harvested in the fall and the people knew they had enough food to last through the next winter they were very pleased. The first Thanksgiving took place and the people gave thanks to God for the harvest. This miniature thanksgiving meal is made from oven-hardening clay. You will need green, buff and orange clay.

You will need:
Oven-hardening clay
Baking tray
Water soluble Varnish
Paintbrush
Thin cardboard
Scissors

1 The miniature turkey and roast potatoes are made from buff colored oven-hardening clay. Shape the turkey's body first then add the drumsticks. Make quite a few roast potato shapes to go around the turkey. Roll out tiny green peas (you will need an awful lot of them!) and carrots from orange clay. Place the pieces on an baking tray and bake according to the manufacturer's instructions.

2 To make the pumpkin pie you will need a layer of buff clay (for the pastry base) and a layer of orange (for the pumpkin filling). You might want to make impressions along the outside edge of the pie to give the look of a pastry case. Place a ball of white clay as cream in the centre of the pie. Bake the pie in the oven according to the manufacturer's instructions.

3 Once your Thanksgiving meal is ready assemble all the pieces on some plates cut from a piece of thin cardboard.

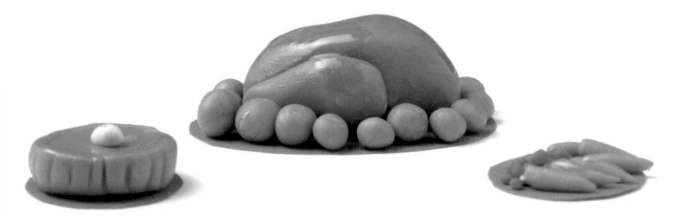

Make your own Craft Box

It is a good idea to store all your craft materials in one place. This keeps things tidy and you always know where your stuff is. You could decorate a large sturdy box and use that. When you have finished working on a project, clean up your equipment and return everything to the box. When you have a spare moment you will be able to get straight down to being creative with all your materials to hand.

A craft box can be made especially useful if you also store found materials in it; things like feathers you may find in the garden or nice shaped pebbles to paint. You can save empty boxes and cans to recycle into interesting birthday or Christmas gifts when you have time. Colored paper is very useful—save used wrapping paper and ribbon. You may want to iron the paper with a cool iron to flatten it ready for reuse.

Plenty of useful craft materials can be found in the summer, interesting seed heads from the garden, and flowers to press. A few twigs and sticks tidily held together with a rubber band could come in useful if a younger sister needs a new piece of furniture for her dollhouse. Ice-cream sticks should be washed, dried, and saved for later. Enjoy collecting interesting materials to recycle into useful gifts, games, and crafts.

Measurements & Recipes

Length	
cm	ins
2.5	1
5	2
7.6	3
10	4
12.7	5
15	6
17.7	7
20	8
22.8	9
25.4	10

Weight	
oz	grams
1	30
3	75
6	175
8	250

Temperature	
Fahrenheit	Centigrade
250–300	120–150
300–350	150–175
350–375	175–190
375–400	190–200
400–425	200–220

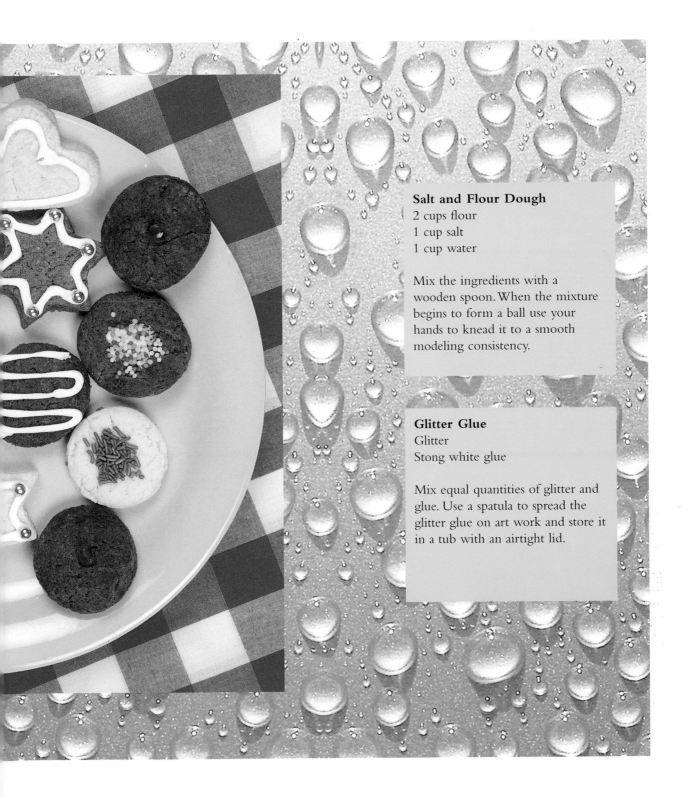

Salt and Flour Dough
2 cups flour
1 cup salt
1 cup water

Mix the ingredients with a
wooden spoon. When the mixture
begins to form a ball use your
hands to knead it to a smooth
modeling consistency.

Glitter Glue
Glitter
Stong white glue

Mix equal quantities of glitter and
glue. Use a spatula to spread the
glitter glue on art work and store it
in a tub with an airtight lid.

Index

Acknowledgments

The publishers would like to thank the children listed below for appearing in the photographs in this book

Fola Akinwumi
Rebecca Anderson
Luke Anderson
Joe Bacon
Matthew Bames-Smith
Natasha Bames-Smith
Laura Bannister
Lauren Barrett
Jenny Beacock
Lillie Berger
Alex Bermingham
Harriet Bolton
Scarlett Bolton
Alice Bolton
Peter Bolton
Ben Boyd
William Brown
Joshua Brown
Leanne Marie Claydon
Killian Collender
Tim Cutting
Donal Edwards
Stephanie Everett
Hazel Garvie-Cook
Joshua George
Katie George
Africa Green
James Grimsaw
Francesca Hails
Joshua Hails
David Haines
Chloe Hannan
Anna Harrington
Lucy Harrington
Ben Howard
Cordell Jackson
Ben Kelvin
Rebecca Kelvin
Jessica Kilpatrick

Jack Kilpatrick
Charlie Mackrill
Abigail Mackrill
James McDonald
Kirsty McDonald
Samuel McGill
Puspita McKenzie
David Merriam
Ned Miles
Vicky Miller
Benedict O'Neill
Luke O'Neill
Ryan Oyeyemi
Holly Rayson
Daisy Rayson
Natalie Roberts
Luke Rutter
Lucy Sales
Eriko Sato
Jamie Saunter
Tariq Sayfoo
Shirine Sayfoo
Julia Smerdon
Katie Smerdon
Lizzie Smith
Christopher Stacey
Emma Stacey
Oliver Sword
Harriet Thomas
Jessica Thurbourn
Helen Thurlow
Rebecca Tomlinson
Joanna Tomlinson
Ava Wallington-Wallis
Sebina Wallis-King
Charlie Wapshott
Tom Wapshott
Andrew Waterhouse
Frances Waterhouse